EYEWITNESS TRAVEL

TOP 10
AMSTERDAM

FIONA DUNCAN
LEONIE GLASS

Top 10 Amsterdam Highlights

The Top 10 of Everything

CONTENTS

Amsterdam Area by Area

Streetsmart

Within each Top 10 list in this book, no hierarchy of quality or popularity is implied. All 10 are, in the editor's opinion, of roughly equal merit.

Front cover and spine *St Nicolaasbasiliek, seen from Oudezijds Voorburgwal Canal*
Back cover *Typical houses and boats lining a canal*
Title page *The splendid Rijksmuseum, a well-known Amsterdam landmark*

Welcome to
Amsterdam

Who could deny Amsterdam's beauty, its lattice of olive-green canals framing some of Europe's most enchanting architecture? Yet the city is no museum piece: Amsterdam sits at the cutting edge of design and has an extraordinarily rich cache of fine art displayed to great advantage in its world-class museums. With Eyewitness Top 10 Amsterdam, its yours to explore.

With every justification, Amsterdam is one of the most popular tourist destinations in Europe and, although many of its visitors come here for the marijuana and the **Red Light District**, the city has so much more to offer. Two of its most prestigious attractions are the internationally famous **Van Gogh Museum** and the **Rijksmuseum**, which, with its magnificent collection of 17th-century Dutch art, is the most visited museum in town. The **Anne Frank House** stands as a solemn reminder of the German occupation of the city during World War II and the persecution of the Jews. These three highlights alone justify a trip to Amsterdam, but the city also boasts a clutch of first-rate restaurants, convivial bars, historic churches – the **Oude Kerk** is the pick – charming hotels, super-charged clubs, a booming gay scene and a bevy of designer shops.

But it's Amsterdam's harmonious cityscapes that are its most distinctive feature. Whatever else you do, take time to stroll the **Grachtengordel**, whose set of concentric canals are interrupted by charming humpback bridges and decorated with handsome mansions built for the merchant elite during the city's 17th-century Golden Age.

Whether you're coming for a weekend or a week, our Top 10 guide brings together the best of everything the city can offer, from historic **Oude Zijde** to bohemian **Jordaan**. With tips throughout, from finding the best bars to getting off the beaten track, plus 10 easy-to-follow itineraries, inspiring photography and detailed maps, it's your essential pocket-sized travel companion to Amsterdam. **Enjoy the book, and enjoy Amsterdam**.

Clockwise from top: Amsterdam skyline, Magere Bruge at dusk, contemporary canal houses, wooden clogs with flowers, bridge over the Singel, Rijksmuseum; St Nicolaasbasiliek

Exploring Amsterdam

Amsterdam is a comparatively small city and good to explore on foot as almost all of the key attractions are close together. However, expect rain at any time, and much of the city centre is cobbled, which can be hard on the feet. Here are some ideas for two and four days of sightseeing.

Brouwersgracht, the "Brewers' Canal", provides a picturesque backdrop for a stroll or canal cruise.

Two Days in Amsterdam

Day ❶

MORNING

Start the morning at the **Anne Frank House** *(see pp38–9)* – bright and early to avoid the crowds. Then pop along to the **Westerkerk** *(see p95)* before wandering at least part of the **Grachtengordel** *(see p15)*.

AFTERNOON

Enjoy the bustle of the **Leidseplein** *(see p105)* as you continue on to the **Rijksmuseum** *(see pp16–19)* with its superb collection of paintings.

Day ❷

MORNING

Start in **Dam Square** *(see pp40–41)* and the **Koninklijk Paleis** *(see p87)*, and then on to the **Red Light District** *(see p81)*, **Oude Kerk** *(see pp34–5)* and **Ons' Lieve Heer op Solder** *(see pp24–5)*.

AFTERNOON

Allow at least an hour or two for the **Van Gogh Museum** *(see pp20–23)*. Alternatively, modern-art lovers can visit neighbouring **Stedelijk Museum** *(see p121)* – those with museum fatigue may prefer to explore the greenery of the **Vondelpark** *(see p121)* instead.

Four Days in Amsterdam

Day ❶

MORNING

Begin the morning with a **canal cruise** *(see pp142–3)* from Stationsplein and then proceed to **Dam Square** *(see pp40–41)*, at the

Van Gogh Museum, a must-visit for art lovers; the world's largest collection of works by the tortured artist is on permanent display here.

Key

— Two-day Itinerary

— Four-day Itinerary

The Rijksmuseum's main building is a familiar Amsterdam landmark.

heart of the city, visiting the **Koninklijk Paleis** (Royal Palace; see p87) and the **Nieuwe Kerk** (see p87).

AFTERNOON

Take lunch on the **Nieuwmarkt** (see p81) before exploring the **Red Light District** (see p81), visiting both the **Oude Kerk** (see pp34–5) and the clandestine church, **Ons' Lieve Heer op Solder** (see pp24–5).

Day ❷
MORNING

Head up to **Brouwersgracht** (see p96) and then stroll through the Grachtengordel (see p15) as the mood suits you. This is the prettiest part of Amsterdam and you can get a flavour for its history at the **Museum Van Loon** (see pp36–7).

AFTERNOON

Set the whole afternoon aside for the **Rijksmuseum** (see pp16–19) with its wonderous collection of Golden Age (Dutch) paintings. Take tea here too.

Day ❸
MORNING

Don't miss the much vaunted **Van Gogh Museum** (see pp20–23) or visit the **Stedelijk Museum** (see p121) of modern art next door. Afterwards, take a stroll through the **Vondelpark** (see p121) and lunch at **Het Blauwe Theehuis** (see p66).

AFTERNOON

Take the tram back to Centraal Station and then catch the ferry over the River IJ to the **EYE Film Institute** (see p131), from where there are great views back over the city.

Day ❹
MORNING

Begin the day at the **Anne Frank House** (see pp38–9) and then drop by the **Westerkerk** (see p95), where Rembrandt was interred, before viewing the quiet charms of the **Begijnhof** (see pp26–7).

AFTERNOON

Spend the afternoon visiting the **Amsterdam Museum** (see pp30–33), which traces the city's history. Time permitting, round off the day at the city's botanical gardens, the **Hortus Botanicus** (see p128).

Top 10 Amsterdam Highlights

Begijnhof courtyard

ᴛᴏᴘ10 Amsterdam Highlights

Amsterdam has an appeal that is absolutely unique. It is a vibrant treasure-trove of extraordinary artistic riches, and the living embodiment of 900 years of history. Elegant and serene, Amsterdam also has its seamy side, as much a part of its charact as its famous network of canals. This small city packs a big punch

1 Canals and Waterways

Amsterdam's canals – in particular, the ring of 17th-century canals known as the Grachtengordel – are its defining feature *(see pp12–15).*

2 Rijksmuseum

The national museum houses an unrivalled collection of 17th-century Dutch art. Star exhibits include Rembrandt's *The Night Watch (see pp16–19).*

3 Van Gogh Museum

The Van Gogh Museum houses simply the most comprehensive collectio of the artist's work to be seen anywhere the world – including some of his most famous paintings *(see pp20–23).*

4 Museum Ons' Lieve Heer op Solder

This fascinating 17th-century house in the Red Light District is a rare example of a perfectly preserved hidden Catholic church *(see pp24–5).*

⑤ Begijnhof

A haven of peace, the Begijnhof was built as a refuge for the Beguines, a lay Catholic sisterhood. Amsterdam's oldest house can be found here *(see pp26–7)*.

⑥ Amsterdam Museum

Housed in the old city orphanage, this vibrant collection traces the city's history from the 12th century *(see pp30–33)*.

⑦ Oude Kerk

This great Gothic basilica retains a number of its treasures, despite being stripped of its paintings and statuary during the Iconoclasm *(see pp34–5)*.

⑧ Museum Van Loon

The Van Loon family residence on the Keizersgracht has been lovingly restored in the style of the mid-18th century *(see pp36–7)*.

⑨ Anne Frank House

The hiding place of Anne Frank and her family, before they were discovered, arrested and sent to their deaths, is today a deeply moving museum *(see pp38–9)*.

⑩ Dam Square

Where it began: Amsterdam's main square is on the site of the dam on the Amstel, around which the city grew *(see pp40–41)*.

🔟 ⭐ Canals and Waterways

With their pretty bridges (1,703 in all), idiosyncratic gabled houses and relaxed waterside cafés, Amsterdam's 75 km (47 miles) of canals are perfect for a leisurely stroll. They are a constant reminder that the Netherlands is the world's flattest country, portions of which have been reclaimed from the sea with the aid of dykes, canals, tidal barriers, and man-made land. Before exploring the canals on foot, take a boat tour *(see pp142–3)* for a fascinating overview. In 2010 the 17th-century canal ring was added to the UNESCO World Heritage List.

1 Herengracht
Stateliest canal of the Grachtengordel *(see p15)*, the elegant Herengracht **(above)** is famous for its Golden Bend – a grand stretch of mansions built for the richest merchants. A more beautiful stretch lies between Huidenstraat and Leidsestraat, best viewed from the east side.

2 Keizersgracht
A central canal of the Grachtengordel **(above)** has fine stretches between Brouwersgracht and Raadhuisstraat, and again between Runstraat and Leidsestraat.

3 Reguliersgracht
Much loved for its pretty canal houses and humpback bridges, Reguliersgracht was cut in 1664. Look out for Nos. 57, 59 and 63.

4 Entrepotdok
An imposing stretch of former dockland has been restored to provide offices and apartments, with outdoor cafés overlooking colourful houseboats.

Prinsengracht 5
The outermost canal of the Grachten-gordel, designed for warehouses and artisans' housing, has a breezy, laid-back air. It is peppered with cafés, art galleries and houseboats. Cycle its 3-km (2-mile) length, or explore short stretches on foot **(right)**.

6 Leidsegracht
This canal **(above)** was cut in 1664 as a barge route to Leiden. Today it is one of the city's most exclusive addresses.

Map of the canals

⑩ ⑤ ⑦ ⑨ ⑥ ③ ❶ ❷ ❹ ❽

JORDAAN NIEUWE
ZIJDE OUDE
ZIJDE PLANTAGE

HOW AMSTERDAM'S HOUSES ARE BUILT

Each house is built on wooden piles sunk into the marshy, porous subsoil. It wasn't until the 17th century, when the piles could be sunk deep enough to reach the hard layer of sand that lies at 13 m (42 ft), that any real stability was achieved. Some reach even further, to a second layer of sand at 18 m (58 ft). If piles come into contact with air, they rot, so today, concrete is used instead of wood.

⑧ Amstel River

Before the construction of the Grachtengordel, the river Amstel was the city's *raison d'être*. It is still used by barges to transport goods to the city's port.

⑨ Singel

The innermost ring of the Grachtengordel, the Singel was originally a moat circling the city during the Middle Ages. In the Golden Age it was lined with canal houses.

⑦ Bloemgracht

Crossed by cast-iron bridges, this is known locally as "the Herengracht of the Jordaan", because of its elaborately gabled houses.

NEED TO KNOW

■ Three perfect canal-side cafés are Papeneiland, at Prinsengracht 2, Van Puffelen, where you can sit on a barge in summer *(see p106)*, and Café de Sluyswacht *(see p84)*.

■ If you are short on time, at least take a stroll to the Huis op de Drie Grachten, (House on Three Canals), step-gabled on all three of its canal-facing sides, at Oudezijds Voorburgwal 249. Afterwards, visit Het Grachtenhuis for a fascinating exhibition on the creation of Amsterdam's canal ring *(see p105)*.

⑩ Brouwersgracht

The happy-go-lucky feel of the "Brewers' Canal" **(above)**, makes a pleasant contrast to the sophisticated elegance of the Grachtengordel.

Unexpected Sights on a Canal Tour

The exterior of the Dutch National Bank building

1 The Dutch National Bank

The vaults of the Dutch National Bank are sunk some 15 m (48 ft) below ground level. In the event of an alarm, they have been designed to allow the waters of the Singelgracht to flood into them.

2 The Prison Bridge

The Torensluis – the widest bridge in the city – spans the Singel on the site of a 17th-century tower. A lock-up jail, sometimes open to the public, was built into its foundations.

3 The Cat Boat

Hundreds of feline waifs and strays are given refuge in De Poezenboot (The Cat Boat), moored on the Singel.

4 The Drunken Tsar

In 1716, Peter the Great got drunk at his friend Christoffel Brants' house at Keizersgracht 317, and kept the mayor waiting at a civic reception. That night, he stayed at the house of the Russian ambassador, Herengracht 527, where Napoleon stayed in 1811.

5 The Narrowest House

Singel 7: the smallest house in Amsterdam? No, it's the back door of a wedge-shaped house.

6 Blue Angel

Cast your eye upwards to the beautiful Blue Angel statue perched on the former Levensverzekering Maatschappij - Noord-Braband building, at the corner of Singel and Haarlemmerstraat.

7 The Most Crooked Café

Teetering Café de Sluyswacht, built in 1695, makes an alarming sight as you glide by along the Oudeschans (see p84).

8 The Wrapped-up House

Look carefully at Victoria Hotel, near the station, and you will see two tiny 17th-century houses in the monumental 19th-century façade. A little old lady, so the story goes, refused to sell up, so the hotel had to wrap itself around them.

9 Museumhaven, Oosterdok

The long jetty leading up to the elevated hood above the River IJ is lined with vintage boats and barges dating from the 19th century.

10 The Tower of Tears

Originally part of the medieval city wall, this 15th-century tower has the saddest of names: Schreierstoren, from where weeping women waved farewell to their seafaring men.

THE GRACHTENGORDEL

Declared a UNESCO World Heritage Site in 2010, Amsterdam's magnificent semicircle of four canals – the Singel, Herengracht, Keizersgracht, and Prinsengracht – is the city's defining characteristic. Lined by elegant gabled houses, and connected by intimate cross-streets, the three outer canals were devised in the early 17th century to cope with the rapid rise in population. Previously a moat, the Singel was now considered a part of the ring as houses were built on it during this period. Built in two stages, this costly plan was purely aesthetic – the land along the banks was sold in single, long plots that were taxed on width; the wealthy bought two together.

Amsterdam had its unlikely beginnings some 400 years earlier, when a fishing settlement grew up on the marshy banks of the river Amstel. (It was dammed in 1222 – hence the name, a contraction of Amstelledamme.) As the town began to expand, canals were cut to drain more land and provide transport channels; the outer canals were fortified. A glance at a map clearly shows the limits of the medieval town, bounded by the curved Singel, with the rest of the Grachtengordel fanning out beyond.

Magere Brug, literally "skinny bridge", was built over the River Amstel in 1934.

TOP 10
BRIDGES

1 Magere Brug (Amstel)

2 Python Bridge

3 Jan Schaefer Bridge

4 Nieuwe Amstelbrug (Amstel)

5 Berlagebrug (Amstel)

6 Torensluis (Singel)

7 St Antoniesluis (Zwanenburgwal)

8 Seven (humpback) bridges (Reguliersgracht)

9 White wooden drawbridges (Western Islands)

10 Sleutelbrug (Oudezijds Voorburgwal)

The Grachtengordel looks its best bathed in dusk light.

TOP 10 ⭐ Rijksmuseum

The magnificent national museum of the Netherlands possesses nearly one million Dutch works of art, only a fraction of which is on display. It was established by King Louis Napoleon in 1808 in the Royal Palace on the Dam, moving to its present location near the Vondelpark in 1885. The main building, designed by P J H Cuypers, underwent extensive renovation for 10 years, reopening in 2013.

The Kitchen Maid **1**

The sense of realism in this painting by Vermeer (c.1658) is conveyed by his mastery of light, colour and perspective. Seen slightly from below against a bare wall, the simple, sturdy girl seems almost tangible – quiet and still, but for the milk flowing from her jug **(right)**.

2 FK23 Bantam

Designed by Frits Koolhoven in 1917, this aeroplane is an icon of the Dutch contribution to aviation, with a fuselage with wooden frames, wooden propeller and wicker pilot's chair.

4 Temple Guard

This depiction of temple guard Naraen Kongo (Ungyo) dates from between 1300 and 1400 and is made from wood with traces of polychromy **(left)**.

6 Our Lady of Sorrows

This unique Flemish terracotta bust (c.1500–1510) is a lifelike depiction of Mary in mourning: the Mater Dolorosa.

5 Two Toilet Caskets

Created by the celebrated Parisian furniture maker, André-Charles Boulle (c.1688), these paired toilet caskets are a fine example of the artist's work, representing the Renaissance styles of tortoiseshell and gilded bronze.

7 Windmill on a Polder Waterway

Paul Joseph Constantin Gabriel's balanced composition **(left)** is heavily influenced by Impressionist ideas, with its use of quick brushstrokes. It was acquired by the Rijksmuseum in 1889 and was considered modern for the time.

3 The Night Watch

Rembrandt's *The Militia Company of Captain Frans Banning Cocq* (1642) – otherwise known as *The Night Watch* – is the museum's prized possession, given pride of place in the Philips Wing.

The Jewish Bride ⑧
In creating one of the most tender portraits ever painted (**right**; 1667), Rembrandt – in an unusually free style – depicts a couple in the guise of biblical characters Isaac and Rebecca.

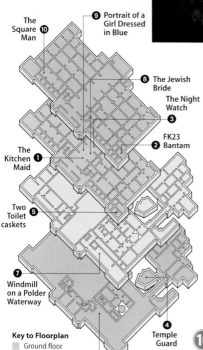

⑨ Portrait of a Girl Dressed in Blue

The Square Man ⑩

⑧ The Jewish Bride

The Night Watch ❸

FK23 Bantam ❷

The Kitchen Maid ❶

Two Toilet caskets ❺

Windmill on a Polder Waterway ❼

Temple Guard ❹

Our Lady of Sorrows ❻

Key to Floorplan
Ground floor
First floor
Second floor
Third floor

Portrait of a Girl Dressed in Blue ⑨
This portrait by Johannes Verspronck (1641) shows the artist's signature style of painting (**below**). Smooth, almost invisible brush strokes contrast with the rougher styles of contemporaries such as Frans Hals (see p48).

⑩ The Square Man
The Square Man (1951) is typical of Karel Appel's work during his CoBrA years, defining the face of Dutch art in this period.

NEED TO KNOW

MAP D5 ■ Museumstraat 1 ■ 020 674 7000 ■ www.rijksmuseum.nl

Open 9am–5pm daily

Adm: €17.50 (under 18s free); garden, shop free

■ The Rijksmuseum Café on the ground floor overlooking the Atrium is a great place to crowd-watch and rest weary feet.

■ With 80 rooms and 8,000 artworks spread over four floors, don't expect to see everything in a single visit. Temporary exhibitions are in the Philips Wing, as well as in the print rooms on every floor of the main building.

Museum Guide
The museum is split into eras, with the Middle Ages, Renaissance, Special

Collections and Asian Pavilion housed on the ground floor; 18th- and 19th-century art on the first floor; 17th-century Golden Age on the second floor; and 20th-century pieces on the third floor. There are two main entrances, all located within the Atrium. One leads to the East wing, and one to the West. Items on display may be moved around the museum.

Rijksmuseum Features

1 **The Building**
The architect P J H Cuypers attracted strong criticism from the Protestant community, who took exception to the building's Neo-Gothic roofs and ornately decorated façade. King William III refused to set foot inside.

2 **The Gardens**
A little-known, immaculate haven, it is studded with statues and architectural curiosities (see p75).

3 **Atrium**
The entrance and heart of the museum, the two courtyards of the Atrium – now restored to their original 1885 condition – are linked by an underground passageway.

4 **Terrazzo Floor**
Covered in 1920 and hacked away in the late 20th century, Cuypers' original terrazzo floor has been restored to its former glory. Hundreds of thousands of small marble stones make up this floor, which is rich in symbolism.

5 **Library**
The library is only open to researchers of art history, but museum visitors can have a look through a large glass wall to view its impressive interior and book collection.

6 **Asian Pavilion**
A quiet, meditative place, this is a wonderful retreat from the swarming masses. Elsewhere, Dutch art proliferates; the Asian Pavilion offers an insight into a different culture, with works spanning 4,000 years from 2000 BC.

Museum Floorplan

Key to Floorplan
- Ground floor
- First floor
- Second floor
- Third floor

7 **Special Collection**
The Special Collection ranges from amusing to bizarre: rooms full of boxes, animals, Meissen porcelain, miniature silver, an armoury, and even the hair of Jacoba of Bavaria, the 15th-century Countess of Holland and Zeeland.

8 **The Golden Age**
Renowned the world over for its 17th-century collection, the Rijksmuseum draws many visitors to see paintings by Dutch Masters such as Rembrandt, Vermeer, Jan Steen and Frans Hals.

9 **Modern Art**
Two loft-like spaces on the third floor house art from the 20th century: one 1900–1950; the other 1950–2000.

10 **Great Hall**
The second-floor Great Hall has been reconstructed to how it looked in Cuypers' day, with elaborate, beautiful late 19th-century decoration.

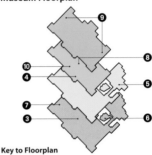
Seated Guanyin, Asian Pavilion

REMBRANDT AND THE NIGHT WATCH

Self-Portrait, **Rembrandt**

Popular belief holds Rembrandt's greatest painting, *The Night Watch* (1642), responsible for his change in fortune from rich man to pauper. In fact, it was more a case of poor personal financial management than of public dissatisfaction with the artist, although it's very likely that the militiamen who commissioned the portrait would have been dismayed at the result. *The Night Watch* differs radically from other contemporary portraits of companies of civic guards, in which they are depicted seated, serious and soberly dressed *(see p32)*. Rembrandt, by contrast, shows a tumultuous scene – the captain issuing orders to his lieutenant, the men taking up arms ready to march. This huge painting was originally even larger, but it was drastically cut down in 1715, when it was moved to the town hall, and tragically the other pieces of the masterpiece were lost. In 1975, the painting was slashed, but was meticulously repaired.

**TOP 10
EVENTS IN
REMBRANDT'S LIFE**

1 Born in Leiden (1606)

2 Studies with Pieter Lastman (1624)

3 Receives first important commission and marries Saskia van Uylenburgh (1634)

4 Reputation grows; buys large house in Amsterdam (1639) – now the Museum Het Rembrandthuis

5 Titus, his only child to survive into adulthood, is born (1641)

6 Saskia dies; *The Night Watch* is completed (1642)

7 Hendrickje Stoffels moves in (1649)

8 Applies for bankruptcy (1656)

9 Titus and Hendrickje acquire the rights to his work

10 Death of Titus (1668); in October the following year, Rembrandt dies

The Night Watch by Rembrandt, was arguably the 17th-century Dutch master's greatest-ever work.

TOP 10 ⭐ Van Gogh Museum

The most comprehensive collection in the world of Van Gogh's work was amassed by his art dealer brother Theo, and is housed in this museum. It includes more than 200 of his paintings, over 500 drawings and hundreds of letters, as well as works by his contemporaries – though not all are on display. The display in Gerrit Rietveld's stunning 1973 building works thematically through Van Gogh's life, his struggles and development as an artist and how he influenced, and was influenced by, other artists.

The Bedroom ①
The mastery of this painting (1888) lies in the simplicity of the subject and the subtly alternating blocks of colour **(right)**. Van Gogh was so happy with the result he made two copies.

② **Almond Blossom**
Van Gogh made this picture of white almond blossom against a blue sky for his new nephew, born in January 1890 and named after him.

③ **The Reaper**
While undergoing treatment in Saint-Rémy, Van Gogh found solace painting people who worked the land. He painted three versions of *The Reaper* (1889).

⑤ **A Pair of Shoes**
Van Gogh gives character to a pair of worn boots in one of the first paintings after his move to Paris (1886). The dark palette harks back to his Nuenen work.

⑥ **Fishing Boats on the Beach at Les Saintes-Maries-de-la-Mer**
A trip to the sea in 1888 produced these colourful, stylized boats. Look closely and you will see grains of sand, blown on to the canvas and fixed there forever as the paint dried.

⑦ **The Potato Eaters**
The culmination of his years in Nuenen, this was Van Gogh's first major composition (1885). He wanted to portray the peasants realistically, not to glamorize them, but the painting was not the critical success he had hoped for.

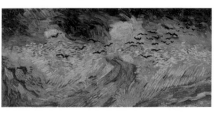

④ **Wheatfield with Crows**
One of the panoramic landscapes that Van Gogh painted in 1890, during the last days of his life, this famous picture with its dead-end track and menacing, crow-filled sky, perhaps reveals his tortured state of mind **(above)**.

Sunflowers

This vibrant painting (1889) was intended to be one of a series of still lifes to fill the "Yellow House" at Arles. Van Gogh chose sunflowers because he was expecting Paul Gauguin, and knew his friend liked them. The predominant yellows and oranges contrast with strokes of brilliant mauve and red **(right)**.

Key to Floorplan

- Temporary exhibitions
- Self-portraits and timeline
- Van Gogh 1883–1889
- Van Gogh close-up
- Van Gogh 1889–1890

Third floor

Second floor

First floor

Basement

Ground floor

9 The Bridge in the Rain

This work, painted in 1887, illustrates Van Gogh's interest in Japanese art, in particular Utagawa Hiroshige. However, Van Gogh used far brighter colours and greater contrasts.

10 Self-Portrait as a Painter

The last and most accomplished in a series of self-portraits painted in 1887, shortly before he left Paris, reveals Van Gogh's distinctive inter-pretation of Pointillism. He chose himself as subject since he could seldom afford models.

NEED TO KNOW

MAP C6 ■ Museumplein ■ 020 570 5200 ■ www. vangoghmuseum.nl/en

Open Apr–mid-Jul & Sep–Nov: 9am–6pm Sat–Thu (mid-Jul–Aug: to 7pm; Dec–Mar: to 5pm), 9am–10pm Fri

Adm: €17 (under 18s free)

Audio tours €5; group tours (up to 15 people) €85, by appointment only

■ The museum has a useful self-service café, which is situated on the ground floor.

■ To avoid the crowds, arrive at opening time or buy tickets on the museum's website. The best times for viewing are at opening or after 3pm. Last admission is 30 minutes before closing.

Museum Guide
Exhibits are displayed on all floors and present the complete story of the artist, his vision, his ideas and ambitions, his influences and the various myths surrounding him. The works are set in the context of other artists of the time. Many of the pivotal paintings form the focus of a theme. Check the latest floorplan at the museum as exhibits are moved around regularly.

Van Gogh Museum: Other Artists

View of Prins Hendrikkade, **Monet**

1 View of Prins Hendrikkade and the Kromme Waal in Amsterdam

Claude Monet painted this cityscape in the winter of 1874 from a boat on the IJ river. Rapid brush strokes loosely recreate the light and feel of the city.

2 Young Peasant Girl with a Hoe

Jules Breton was an idol of Van Gogh. In rural scenes like this one (1882), he places an idealized figure of a peasant girl in a realistic setting.

3 Exhausted Maenads after the Dance

In this Lawrence Alma-Tadema painting of 1874, three devotees (maenads) of the wine god, Bacchus, have fallen asleep.

4 Portrait of Bernard's Grandmother

Van Gogh swapped one of his self-portraits, *Self-Portrait with a Straw Hat,* for this painting (1887) by Emile Bernard, while in Paris.

5 Young Woman at a Table, "Poudre de Riz"

This early painting by Toulouse-Lautrec (1887), who became a friend of Van Gogh, is probably of his mistress, Suzanne Valadon.

6 Portrait of Guus Preitinger, the Artist's Wife

The vivid use of colour in Kees van Dongen's wild, lush portrait of his wife (1911) is characteristic of Fauvism.

7 Self-Portrait with a Portrait of Bernard, "Les Misérables"

In his powerful self-portrait (1888), Paul Gauguin identified himself with the hero of Victor Hugo's *Les Misérables*, Jean Valjean.

8 Saint Geneviève as a Child in Prayer

An oil study (1876) by Puvis de Chavannes for the huge murals he painted at the Panthéon in Paris on the theme of St Geneviève's childhood.

Saint Geneviève as a Child in Prayer, **de Chavannes**

9 "Grand Paysan"

Jules Dalou shared Van Gogh's preoccupation with peasants, whom he saw as heroic labourers. He devised this life-size bronze sculpture in 1889.

10 Two Women Embracing

Van Gogh's influence on the Dutch artist Jan Sluijters is obvious in the brushwork and colour of this painting of 1906.

THE LIFE OF VINCENT VAN GOGH

Self-Portrait,
Van Gogh

Born on 30 March 1853 in Zundert, Vincent Van Gogh was the eldest son of a pastor and his wife. Aged 16, he joined his uncle's business Goupil & Co., art dealers. Seven years later, displaying increasingly erratic behaviour, he was dismissed. After a couple of false starts as teacher and evangelist, in 1880 he decided to be a painter. From 1883 to 1885, he lived with his parents in Nuenen, but in 1886 he went to Paris to study in Fernand Cormon's studio. He lived with his brother Theo, met renowned artists and changed his style. In 1888, he moved to Arles where he dreamed of establishing an artists' colony with Paul Gauguin. Soon after Gauguin arrived, the friends had a fierce argument and, during a psychotic attack, Van Gogh cut off a piece of his own left ear lobe. He enrolled as a voluntary patient in a clinic in Saint-Rémy in 1889. The following year, he left for the rural village Auvers-sur-Oise, where his state of mind deteriorated and he shot himself in the chest on 27 July 1890. He died, with Theo at his bedside, two days later.

**TOP 10
19TH-CENTURY
ARTISTS**

1 Vincent Van Gogh
(1853–1890)

2 Claude Monet
(1840–1926)

3 Pierre Auguste Renoir
(1841–1919)

4 Paul Cézanne
(1839–1906)

5 Auguste Rodin
(1840–1917)

6 Edouard Manet
(1832–83)

7 Edgar Degas
(1834–1917)

8 J M W Turner
(1775–1851)

9 Eugène Delacroix
(1798–1863)

**10 Jean-Baptiste
Camille Corot**
(1796–1875)

The Yellow House
(1888) was the abode Van Gogh had hoped to share with Gauguin.

TOP 10 ⭐ Museum Ons' Lieve Heer op Solder

Contrasting sharply with its surroundings in the Red Light District, this 17th-century house has, concealed in its upper floors, a church. It is a rare, perfectly preserved example of the many clandestine churches built after the Alteration. Local Catholics worshipped here from 1663 to 1887. Its little-changed interiors transport you back to the Dutch Golden Age. The museum was restored and expanded to include another building in 2011, which now forms the main entrance, and houses a café and exhibition space.

The Hidden Church 1

At the top of the stairs, the *huiskerk* (house church), Ons' Lieve Heer op Solder (Our Lord in the Attic), is a charming sight **(right)**. In c.1735, it was remodelled in Baroque style, with the addition of two tiers of galleries, suspended from the roof by cast-iron rods, to provide extra seating.

2 The Confessional

In 1739, this living room in the middle of the three houses became the church's confessional. One of the two wooden confessional boxes still remains **(left)**.

3 The Maria Chapel and Peat Room

This chapel comprises a small altar dedicated to the Virgin Mary. The statue is one of the few original objects belonging to the 17th-century church.

5 The Sael

Adhering to strict rules of proportion and symmetry, the family's *sael* (formal parlour) is a superb example of the Dutch Classical style fashionable in the 17th century. It is this room the family would have used to receive guests.

4 The Priest's Room

Formerly the servants' quarters, the Priest's Room is in a corner on a bend in the stairs. It's a tiny, enclosed bedroom with a box bed, simply furnished as it would have been for the priest, who lived in the house **(above)**.

6 Canal Room

This 17th-century living room overlooks the canal to the front, and is where residents would spend most of their time during the day. It is decorated with authentic furnishings from the era, including a replica stove.

Key to Floorplan

- Ground floor
- First floor
- Second floor
- Third floor
- Fourth floor
- Fifth floor

7 The Rear Houses

The rear houses were gradually taken over by the church, but there are still signs of their original use as family rooms.

THE ALTERATION

The revolt of the (Calvinist) Northern Netherlands against the (Catholic) Spanish Habsburgs began in 1568, but it was not until 1578 when Amsterdam joined William of Orange in a peaceful revolution known as the Alteration. Calvinists seized power and the city became the Protestant capital of an infant Dutch Republic. Catholics couldn't worship in public, but Dutch tolerance ensured that they were able to continue in private.

8 The Building

The spout-gabled canal house was built in 1661 for Jan Hartman, a Catholic merchant. He combined its attic with the attics of two smaller houses behind to create the hidden church, which was extended in c.1735.

9 The Folding Pulpit

The ingenious pulpit was designed to fold away under the left column of the altar when not in use. The painting above the altar is *The Baptism of Christ* by Jacob de Wit (1695–1754).

NEED TO KNOW

MAP P2 ■ Oudezijds Voorburgwal 38
■ 020 624 6604
■ www.opsolder.nl

Open 10am–6pm Mon–Sat, 1–6pm Sun, public hols; closed 27 Apr

Adm: €10, children 5–18 €5

■ The audio tour is free, and for an extra €1 there is a Ladybird in the Attic tour for kids.

■ No wheelchair access. A virtual tour in the annexe can be arranged.

■ There's a museum shop and café.

■ Sunday Mass is on 1st Sunday of the month.

10 The Kitchen

Once part of the sacristan's secret living quarters, the charming 17th-century kitchen **(left)** has original Delft wall tiles, an open hearth, stone sink and black-and-white floor.

TOP 10 ⭐ Begijnhof

This bewitching sanctuary of elegant houses around a tranquil green was founded in 1346 for the members of a lay Catholic sisterhood, the Beguines, the last of whom died in 1971. Although no original buildings survive, nor the early design of the courtyard surrounded by water, there is a fascinating 15th-century wooden house, a lovely church of the same period and an appealing hidden chapel. Visitors are asked to respect the privacy of the current residents.

① Engelse Kerk

Before the Alteration (see p25), the Beguines worshipped in this pretty 15th-century church (above). Confiscated in 1578, it was let to a group of English and Scottish Presbyterians in 1607, who renamed it the "English Church".

② The Beguine in the Gutter

To make amends for her family's conversion to Protestantism, Cornelia Arents requested in her will not to be buried in the church, but in the gutter outside. Legend has it that her coffin was left inside the church on 2 May 1654, but the following day it was found outside, where she was eventually buried.

③ 17th- and 18th-Century Houses

After several devastating fires, most of the existing houses were built in the 17th and 18th centuries (right). They are typically tall and narrow, with large sash windows and spout or neck gables. The sisterhood owned them, so if a Beguine left or died, outsiders could not claim her house. Today, they provide homes for 100 or so single women.

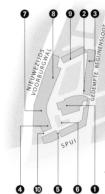

④ Het Houten Huis

No. 34, Het Houten Huis, is one of the oldest houses in Amsterdam (below), and one of only two wood-fronted houses in the city. It predates the 1521 ban on the construction of wooden houses, introduced to reduce the risk of fire.

Plan of Begijnhof

⑤ Spui Entrance

Members of the public use the arched entrance from Gedempte Begijnensloot, but be sure to peep discreetly into the pretty vaulted and tiled passageway leading to Spui.

6 **Statue of a Beguine**

The statue by Engelse Kerk shows a Beguine dressed in a traditional *falie* (headdress) and long garment of undyed cloth.

9 **Wall Plaque on No. 19**

The story depicted on this handsome plaque illustrates the return from Egypt to Israel of Jesus, Mary and Joseph after the death of Herod.

THE WELFARE SYSTEM

Charity lies at the heart of Amsterdam's long tradition of caring for the poor and needy, which goes back to the Middle Ages. In the 14th century, primary responsibility for social welfare passed from the church to the city authorities. They distributed food to the poor, and set up institutions to care for orphans, the sick and the insane. In the 17th century, a number of wealthy merchants funded *hofjes* (almshouses) that provided subsidized mass housing for the city's needy.

7 **Begijnhof Chapel**

The city's first hidden chapel **(below)** was created in 1665, when the Beguines converted two ordinary houses into a little church *(see pp24–5)*. The Miracle of Amsterdam *(see p44)* is commemorated here.

10 **Courtyard with Wall Plaques**

Set into the wall of the courtyard behind Het Houten Huis is a collection of wall plaques from demolished houses. In keeping with the religious nature of the Beguines, each one tells a biblical story.

NEED TO KNOW

MAP M4 ▪ Spui (entrance on Gedempte Begijnensloot) ▪ 020 622 1918 ▪ www.begijnhof amsterdam.nl

Open 9am–5pm daily

Begijnhof Chapel: open 1–6:30pm Mon, 9am–6:30pm Tue–Fri, 9am–6pm Sat–Sun

▪ Café Luxembourg and traditional Café Hoppe are just round the corner in Spui (at Nos. 18 and 24 respectively).

▪ Services are held in Dutch (daily) and French (Sundays) in the Roman Catholic Begijnhof Chapel. Services in English are held in the Protestant Engelse Kerk (Sundays).

▪ Enjoy a concert at the Engelse Kerk.

▪ Pick up an information booklet from Het Houten Huis.

8 **Mother Superior's House**

The grandest house, No. 26, belonged to the Mother Superior. In the 20th century, the last of the Beguines lived together here.

Following pages Houses on the Damrak

TOP 10 ⭐ Amsterdam Museum

The Amsterdam Museum houses the city's collection of artifacts, archaeological finds, clothes, jewellery, maps, paintings and sculptures that chart Amsterdam's metamorphosis over the centuries. Originally a convent, in 1580 it became the city orphanage. Extensions were added by Hendrick and Pieter de Keyser before Jacob van Campen's magnificent rebuilding of 1634. The orphans moved out in 1960; in 1975 the museum moved in.

1 Terrestrial and Celestial Globes

A pair of costly globes lent prestige to any self-respecting 17th-century intellectual. Joan Willemsz Blaeu must have made this unique pair after 1644 because they show the Australian coast, just discovered by Abel Tasman (see p45).

2 Turbo Shell

This exquisite mother-of-pearl *Turbo marmoratus* is covered in tiny engraved animals (above). It dates from c.1650 and was probably brought from the Orient by the Dutch East India Company (VOC).

3 Dam Square with the New Town Hall under Construction

This 1656 snapshot of the Dam by Johannes Lingelbach (above) exudes a bustling energy.

4 Ceremonial Keys to the City

Two gold and silver keys, made by Diederik Lodewijk Bennewitz, were presented by the mayor to Emperor Napoleon on his first and only visit in October 1811.

5 De Witkar

Take a virtual drive in "De Witkar" (The White Car). Luud Schimmelpennink's idea, conceived around 1970, was one of the first car-share projects in the world. The electric cars are unlocked with a magnetic key.

6 Wedding Rings of Amsterdam's First Married Gay Couple

The Netherlands was the first country in the world to legalize same-sex marriage, with the first ceremony of four couples taking place in 2001. These rings were worn by one of these couples.

7 Bird's-Eye View of Amsterdam

Cornelis Anthonisz's 1538 map of Amsterdam (the oldest extant) shows the Dam, Oude Kerk and Nieuwe Kerk (left).

Civic Guardsmen of the Company of Captain Albert Coenraetsz Burgh and Lieutenant Pieter Evertsz Hulft **8**

This oil painting **(right)** by Werner Jacobsz van den Valckert (1625) shows merchant and dyer Albert Burgh keeping watch over Amsterdam's harbour.

Turbo Shell **2**

5 De Witkar

Key to Floorplan
- Ground floor
- First floor
- Second floor

1 Terrestrial and Celestial Globes

9 The Gouden Leeuw on the IJ by Amsterdam

4 Ceremonial Keys to the City

6 Wedding Rings of Amsterdam's First Married Gay Couple

10 Dr F M Wibaut

3 Dam Square

8 The Anatomy Lesson of Dr Jan Deijman

7 Bird's-Eye View of Amsterdam

Dr F M Wibaut **10**

This powerful bronze head **(above)** was made in 1934 by Tjipke Visser, favourite sculptor of the Social Democratic Workers' Party (SDAP). The subject was Floor Wibaut, SDAP Councillor for housing in the 1920s, who dedicated himself to building new apartments for the working class.

The Gouden Leeuw on the IJ by Amsterdam **9**

Willem van de Velde's painting (1686) shows the Gouden Leeuw with a view of Amsterdam across the IJ.

NEED TO KNOW

MAP M4 ▪ Kalverstraat 92; Sint Luciënsteeg 27 ▪ 020 523 1822 ▪ www. amsterdammuseum.nl

Open 10am–5pm Mon–Sun; closed 1 Jan, 27 Apr, 25 Dec

Adm: €13.50 (under 18s free)

▪ Café Mokum is inside Joost Bilhamer's Kalverstraat entrance.

▪ The 45-minute Amsterdam DNA is a must (see p32).

▪ Don't miss the delightful façade stones set into the wall of the museum in St Luciënsteeg.

Museum Guide
Amsterdam DNA – the story of the city from its beginnings as a trading port to the modern day – is housed on the first floor. "Het Kleine Weeshuis" (The Little Orphanage) is on the ground floor, portraying the museum's former life. The permanent exhibition is displayed on all three floors, with a temporary exhibition space on the ground floor. The Civic Guards Gallery is located by the entrance. There is wheelchair access at the St Luciënsteeg entrance.

Amsterdam Museum Rooms

Regents' Chamber, decorated as it was in the 17th century

1 Regents' Chamber
The orphanage governors met in this 17th-century room, maintained in the original Old Holland style.

2 Civic Guard Gallery
This glassed-over gallery displays Amsterdam group portraits – from famous Dutch footballers to the city's 17th-century militia.

3 Temporary Exhibition Space
Once used to house a girls' refectory and needlework rooms, it is now used for temporary exhibitions.

4 Room 0.5: Turbulent Times
Displays from the late 16th century include the Civic Guard's Italian-made armour, and silver that escaped melting down for "crisis coins" in 1578.

5 Room 0.3: The Dam
The bustling heart of the city was a popular subject in 17th-century paintings like Lingelbach's *Dam Square with the New Town Hall under Construction*.

6 Amsterdam DNA
This 3D exhibition takes visitors on a 45-minute historical tour of Amsterdam, telling the multifaceted story of the city.

7 Room 1.4: The 18th Century
The 18th century saw the decline of Amsterdam and, ultimately, the Republic's defeat by the French. A highlight is the museum's collection of 18th-century miniature silver toys.

8 Room 15: 19th-Century Cabinet
There was a 19th-century trend for rich industrialists to collect art. These important collections helped establish the public ownership of art.

9 Room 2.1: Amsterdam 1940–1945
A room devoted to memorabilia of the German occupation.

10 Room 2.4: Café 't Mandje
A reconstruction of leather-clad motorbiker Bet van Beeren's famous café on Zeedijk – the first where patrons could be openly gay.

Museum Floorplan

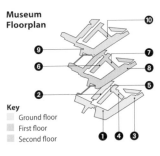

Key
Ground floor
First floor
Second floor

THE GOLDEN AGE

The economic boom of the 17th century laid the foundations for the flowering of the arts in Amsterdam. Plans were laid to surround the city with a triple ring of canals lined with fine houses, a project which required the work of many architects. The most powerful city in the Dutch Republic recognized the importance of the arts, and rewarded its artists well – and with the supremacy of the Protestants came the freedom to paint secular subjects. To show their wealth and status, rich patrons commissioned portraits of themselves and their families. The artists' best clients, however, were the municipal bodies such as the guilds, who commissioned group portraits, as well as decorative pieces of silver and glass. Painters began to focus their energies on a single area of painting – whether historical, portraiture, interiors, genre, still lifes, urban scenes, landscapes or seascapes – and this specialization greatly enhanced the quality of their workmanship.

The Silver Marriage Cup features a hinged bowl above the woman's head and one formed by her full skirt. Once the wedding was in full swing, the bride and groom would down both together.

TOP 10
HIGHLIGHTS OF THE GOLDEN AGE

1 *The Night Watch* by Rembrandt (1642, Rijksmuseum) *(see p19)*

2 **The Grachtengordel** designed by Hendrick Staets (begun in 1613) *(see p15)*

3 **Ons' Lieve Heer op Solder** (1663) *(see pp24–5)*

4 **Westerkerk** by Hendrick de Keyser (1631) *(see p95)*

5 **Huis met de Hoofden** built by Hendrick de Keyser and his son Pieter (1622) *(see p95)*

6 **Claes Claeszhofje** (1616)

7 **Silver Marriage Cup** by Gerrit Valck (1634)

8 **Café Hoppe** (c.1670) *(see p90)*

9 **Delftware** (second half 17th century)

10 **Burgerzaal**, Koninklijk Paleis *(see p40)*

Dutch Battle Ships **by Ludolf Backhuysen**

TOP 10 ⭐ Oude Kerk

The city's oldest monument and first parish church stands on the site of an early 13th-century wooden chapel that was destroyed by fire. Rebuilt as a small stone hall church in the 14th century, over the years it expanded into a mighty Gothic basilica, now in the heart of the Red Light District. The interior boasts some exquisite stained glass, rare ceiling paintings, and a world-famous organ and regularly hosts art exhibitions, performances and debates. It is dedicated to St Nicholas, patron saint of the city.

3 Stained Glass of the Burgemeesters

The colourful stained-glass windows flanking the chancel depict the arms of the city burgomasters from 1578 to 1807 **(left)**. One was designed by De Angeli in 1758; the other by Pieter Jansz in 1654.

1 Spire

From the graceful late-Gothic spire, built by Joost Bilhamer in 1565, there are splendid views over the Oude Zijde. The tower contains a 47-bell carillon, a 17th-century addition that rings out every Saturday afternoon.

4 Great Organ

With its eight pairs of bellows, magnificent oak-encased pipework, marbled wood statues and gilded carving, the great organ is a glorious sight. Built by Christian Vater in 1724 and renovated by Johann Caspar Müller 14 years later, it is known as the Vater-Müller organ.

Oude Kerk

5 Red Door into the Old Sacristy

Rembrandt famously passed through this door to announce his marriage. "Marry in haste, repent at leisure" is inscribed above it.

6 Little Organ

Attractively painted shutters form the original casing built in 1658 – however, the pipework was replaced in 1965. It is tuned as it would have been before 1700, so early Baroque music can now be part of the organist's repertoire.

2 Ceiling

The massive wooden vaulted ceiling **(below)** is claimed to be the largest in Western Europe, but it was only during restoration work in 1955 that the beautiful 15th-century paintings were revealed.

Plan of Oude Kerk

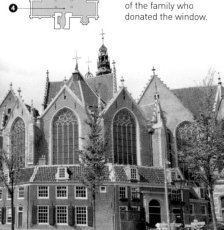

7 Maria Kapel

The most stunning stained glass is in the three windows of the Lady Chapel. All date from the 16th century; two show scenes from the Virgin's life, above the customary picture of the family who donated the window.

THE ICONOCLASM OF 1566

In the 1566 Iconoclasm, or *Beeldenstorm* – precursor to the Alteration of 1578 (see p25) when the city became Protestant – the Calvinists looted Catholic churches and destroyed their treasures, among them the Oude Kerk's pictures, altars and statues. Only the ceiling paintings and stained glass were spared, as they were out of reach. The Calvinists also disapproved of the beggars and pedlars who gathered in the church, and threw them out, ending its role as a city meeting place.

---

8 Saskia's Grave

Among the great and the good buried here is Saskia van Uylenburgh, Rembrandt's first wife, who died in 1642. Her grave is number 29K in the Weitkopers Kapel.

NEED TO KNOW

MAP P2 ■ Oudekerksplein 23
■ 020 625 8284 ■ www.oudekerk.nl

Open 10am–6pm Mon–Sat, 1–5:30pm Sun; closed 27 Apr

Adm: €10; students €7.50 (separate charge for exhibitions)

Guided tours by appointment; www.westertorenamsterdam.nl.

■ For food and peoplewatching, head for Nieuwmarkt; In de Waag (Nieuwmarkt 4) is recommended.

■ Go to the Dutch Reformed Church service at 11am Sunday, or a concert or contemporary art exhibition.

■ Don't miss the votive ships hanging from the choir ceiling.

9 Decorated Pillars

Pre-1578 relics, these pillars **(above)** once supported niches for statues of the Apostles destroyed in the Iconoclasm, and were painted to look like brocade, since the real thing was unsuited to the church's humidity.

10 Misericords

The 15th-century misericords helped choristers take the weight off their feet. Their charming carvings illustrate traditional Dutch proverbs.

📕🔟⭐ Museum Van Loon

Step back into the 18th century at this delightful canal house on Keizersgracht, which has been the property of the prestigious Van Loon family (co-founders of the Dutch East India Company, later bankers and royal courtiers) since 1884. In 1973, the family who still reside here, opened it to the public, having painstaking restored it to its appearance in the 1750s, when it was owned by Dr Abraham van Hagen and his heiress wife, Catharina Trip. It is beautifully furnished with Van Loon family possessions througho

The Garden Room

1 The Building

In 1672, Jeremias van Raey built two large houses on Keizersgracht **(above)**. One he occupied, the other – No. 672, now the Museum Van Loon – he rented to Rembrandt's most famous pupil, Ferdinand Bol.

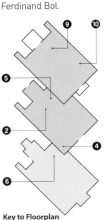

2 The Staircase

The balustrade was installed by Dr Van Hagen, who had his and his wife's names incorporated into the ornate brass work **(right)**. When the canals ceased to freeze over regularly, the 18th-century sledge in the hall became a plant stand.

3 The Coach House

The restored coach house has the family's original coach and livery on display. Temporary exhibitions are held here.

4 The Dining Service

Rare 18th-century D porcelain and 19th-century Limoges wa grace the dining roo

Key to Floorplan
- Ground floor
- First floor
- Second floor

7 The Garden

Laid out according to a plan of the property from 1700, the peaceful, sculptural garden ends in the false Neo-Classical façade of the coach house **(left)**. This original amalgamation of canal house, coach house and garden can be seen nowhere else.

8 The Family Portraits

Portraits of the family **(below)** are displayed throughout the house.

9 The Painted Room

Painted wall hangings such as the ones in this room, featuring ruins, Classical buildings and human figures, were very popular in the 1700s.

NEED TO KNOW

MAP E5
■ Keizersgracht 672
■ 020 624 5255 ■ www. museumvanloon.nl

Open 10am–5pm daily; closed 1 Jan, 27 Apr, 25 Dec

Adm: €9; concessions €7

Guided tours on request.

■ There is a small café in the coach house that serves coffee, tea and wonderful apple cake.

■ Serene and elegant, the Museum Van Loon makes a perfect visit for adults, but not so suited to children. There is no wheelchair access.

Museum Guide
Visitors are welcomed as guests in a private house and encouraged to wander around freely. Temporary exhibitions of modern art and sculpture are displayed in the house, garden and the coach house. The museum also participates in the **Open** Garden Days in June.

5 The Wedding Portrait

Golden Age painter Jan Molenaer's first major commission in Amsterdam portrays the whole family. It's a second marriage: the bride holds her stepson's hand in acceptance, while the fallen chair symbolizes the groom's deceased brother.

6 The Kitchen

Cosy and inviting, the basement kitchen has been restored to look as it did in a photograph from 1900 **(right)**.

10 The Romantic Double Portrait

Painted by J F A Tischbein in 1791, this intimate, relaxed portrait of these Van Loon ancestors is typical of the Age of Enlightenment, conveying love and happiness as well as duty.

TOP 10 ⭐ Anne Frank House

This deeply moving museum tells a tragic story. When, in 1942, the Nazis began to round up Jews in Amsterdam, the Frank and Van Pels families went into hiding. For 25 months, they hid in a secret annexe in the Anne Frank House. In August 1944, they were arrested and deported. Only Otto survived. The diary of his daughter Anne, who died in Bergen-Belsen concentration camp in February 1945 at the age of 15, has made her one of the most inspiring figures of the 20th century. The ever-popular museum attracts more than a million visitors each year.

1 The Warehouse

Otto Frank's business made pectin for jam, and spice and herb mixtures. The annexe was over his warehouse **(below)**; the families had to keep quiet for fear that the workers would hear them.

2 The Offices

Upstairs are the offices of Otto Frank and the staff who helped to hide him and his family, along with Otto's business partner, Hermann van Pels, and his wife and son. In Anne's diary, the Van Pels became the Van Daans.

3 The Moveable Bookcase

To hide the entrance to the annexe, one of the helpers made a swinging bookcase **(right)**. As Anne wrote, "no one could ever suspect that there could be so many rooms hidden behind..."

4 Anne's Room

Film-star pin-ups still adorn the wall of Anne's room **(right)**. After Margot moved in with her parents, Anne had to share this space with a new member of the group, a dentist called Fritz Pfeffer – in Anne's first estimation, "a very nice man".

5 The Secret Annexe

The claustrophobic rooms in which the eight lived have been left unfurnished, as they were when cleared of possessions by the Germans after their arrest. On one wall, pencil marks record the growth of Anne and her sister, Margot.

6 Peter's Room

The small refuge of Peter van Pels **(right)** was the room behind the attic. Anne often spent time here talking with Peter.

7 The Front Attic

In a moving display in the front attic, visitors learn the fate of each member of the group after they were betrayed to the Nazis. Tragically, Anne and Margot Frank died shortly before Bergen-Belsen concentration camp was liberated.

8 The Diary Room

As well as the now famous diary **(above)**, Anne wrote short stories and ideas for novels. As time went on, she began to edit her original diary with a book called *The Secret Annexe* in mind.

ANNE FRANK'S DIARY

On the day the family were taken away, Miep Gies, who had helped conceal them, found Anne's diary. With the words "Here is your daughter Anne's legacy to you", she handed it to Otto Frank on his return from Auschwitz. He prepared a transcript, and the diary was published to great acclaim in the Netherlands in 1947, and in Britain and the United States in 1952. It has since been published in more than 70 languages.

Key to Floorplan
- Ground Floor
- First Floor
- Second Floor
- Third Floor
- Attic

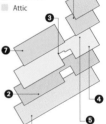

9 Otto Frank Exhibit

An interview with Otto Frank from 1967 and documents from his personal collection are on show. A notebook of entries made after Otto's return from Auschwitz is most poignant.

10 The Exhibition Room

The multimedia exhibition space screens *Reflections on Anne Frank*, a film in which 22 writers, actors, museum visitors and those who knew her talk about what she meant to them.

8 9 10 in separate building

NEED TO KNOW

MAP L2 ■ Westermarkt
■ 020 556 7105
■ www.annefrank.org

Open Nov–Mar: 9am–7pm daily; Apr–Oct: 9am–10pm daily; closed Yom Kippur (Check website for other exceptions)

Adm: €10; children 10–17 €5; under 10s free

A 360 degree virtual reality tour is available for the disabled.

■ There is a pleasant, airy café, with a great view of the Westerkerk.

■ The museum is undergoing renovation work until 2019 and during this time tickets must be booked in advance online.

■ Take care around the house as the stairs are steep and narrow.

■ The visit is a moving experience, so plan something contemplative afterwards: climb the Westerkerk spire, or walk to the Western Islands.

★ Dam Square

The very heart of Amsterdam, Dam Square – or "the Dam", as the locals call it – marks the site of the original 13th-century dam on the Amstel river. By the 17th century, with the town hall here and the Exchange nearby, the Dam had become the focus of Amsterdam's political and commercial life. An architectural parade spanning six centuries includes the glorious Nieuwe Kerk and the Koninklijk Paleis. The passage of years may have eroded some of its grandeur – but none of its colour or vitality.

1 Madame Tussauds Amsterdam

Displays at this outpost of the London waxworks range from the fascinating to the bizarre. Special effects, including animatronics, bring to life scenes from Holland's past **(above)**.

5 Koninklijk Paleis

Built as the town hall, Jacob van Campen's unsmiling Classical edifice symbolizes the worldly power of 17th-century Amsterdam. The Royal Palace is still used by the Dutch Royal House for state occasions *(see p87)*, but is otherwise open to visitors to discover its rich history and interior.

2 Street Performances and Events

Busking, mime acts, funfairs, book fairs, exhibitions, concerts – such things have gone on in the Dam **(right)** since J Cabalt introduced his puppet show in 1900.

3 Damrak

Damrak was once the medieval city's busiest canal, with ships sailing up to be unloaded at the Dam. In 1672, the canal was partially filled in, and Damrak became the shopping strip it is today **(below)**.

4 Nationaal Monument

This 22-m (70-ft)-tall obelisk commemorates the Dutch killed in World War II. Embedded in the wall behind are urns containing soil from the Dutch provinces and overseas colonies.

6 De Bijenkorf

De Bijenkorf (which literally translates as "the beehive") is Amsterdam's most famous high-end department store. It boasts a vast perfumery, designer fashion boutiques and much more.

7 Kalverstraat
Music shops jostle with both tacky and trendy clothes stores at the Dam end of this pedestrian shopping street.

8 Rokin
The Rokin had its heyday in the 19th century, when its broad sweep was a promenade for the well-to-do.

INSIDE THE KONINKLIJK PALEIS

The ponderous exterior belies the magnificent interior – especially the dramatic Burgerzaal (Citizen's Hall). See fine sculptures by Artus Quellien and Rombout Verhulst, ceilings and friezes by Rembrandt's pupils, and Empire furniture owned by Louis Napoleon. The Vierschaar (Tribunal) is a macabre room, still intact, where judges once pronounced the death sentence.

10 Nieuwe Kerk
Now a venue for exhibitions, the Nieuwe Kerk **(left)** has hosted royal events since 1814. Treasures include a Jacob van Campen organ case and an elaborately carved pulpit by Albert Vinckenbrinck *(see p87).*

Plan of Dam Square

9 Grand Hotel Krasnapolsky
Adolf Wilhelm Krasnapolsky, an emigré Polish tailor with ambition, rented the down-at-heel Nieuwe Poolsche Koffiehuis in the 1870s, swiftly transforming it into a fashionable hotel **(left).**

NEED TO KNOW

Madame Tussauds Amsterdam: **MAP N3**; 020 522 1010; open 10am–7pm daily, closed 27 April; Adm €23.50, children 5–15 €19.50, under 5s free, €4 discount when booked online; www.madame tussauds.nl

Koninklijk Paleis: **MAP M3**; 020 522 6161; open 10am–5pm daily (except state functions); Adm: €10, seniors/students €9, under 18s free; www.paleis amsterdam.nl

Nieuwe Kerk: **MAP M3**; 020 638 6909; open during exhibitions: 10am–5pm daily; Adm; www.nieuwekerk.nl

■ Eat at the cafés in de Bijenkorf or the Nieuwe Kerk – the latter's terrace overlooks the Dam.

■ Go to one of the concerts or exhibitions held at the Nieuwe Kerk.

The Top 10
of Everything

The colourful ceiling and Neo-Baroque
dome of St Nicolaasbasiliek

🔟 Moments in Amsterdam's History

1 c.1125: First Settlers

Fishermen settled at the mouth of the Amstel river, building huts on man-made mounds called *terps* for flood protection. With the growth of the new settlement came feudal conflict between the self-made Counts of Holland and Lords van Amstel.

2 1275: Freedom from Tolls

In the earliest document to refer to Amsterdam, Count Floris V of Holland granted its citizens exemption from tolls when transporting their goods by river, leading to the first charter in 1300.

3 1345: Miracle of Amsterdam

At a house in Kalverstraat, a priest gave a dying man the last sacraments. Unable to keep the communion wafer down, he regurgitated it onto the fire. Next morning, the wafer was found intact among the embers. News of the miracle spread, and Amsterdam soon became a place of pilgrimage.

4 1566 and 1578: Iconoclasm and Alteration

As Protestantism swept northern Europe, Dutch Calvinists rebelled against their intolerant Spanish Catholic ruler, Felipe II. In the *Beeldenstorm* or Iconoclasm, the Calvinists stormed the Catholic churches and destroyed their religious artifacts. The city finally became Protestant, in a peaceful revolution known as the *Alteratie* or Alteration *(see p25)*.

Tulipmania

5 1609: Plans for the Grachtengordel

The dawn of the Golden Age, when the arts flourished in Amsterdam *(see p33)*, saw ambitious plans for a triple canal ring around the city *(see p15)*. Herengracht, Keizersgracht and Prinsengracht were built in two stages, with the Singel later considered part of the ring.

6 1634–1637: Tulipmania

The Dutch passion for tulips dates from the late 16th century, when the first bulbs were imported from Asia. In 1634, the tulip was quoted on the Stock Exchange, and speculation began. Fortunes were made overnight as the craze led to spectacular price increases; the inevitable crash caused scores of bankruptcies.

7 1806: Kingdom of the Netherlands Established

After the formation of the Batavian Republic in 1795, rule was shared between

Louis Napoleon

the invading French and the Dutch Patriots. In 1806, Napoleon Bonaparte took over the Republic, created the Kingdom of the Netherlands and installed his brother, Louis Napoleon, as head of state.

8 1940–1945: German Occupation

Despite Dutch neutrality, Germany invaded Holland in May 1940. With the deportation of Jews to concentration camps from 1942 onwards, the Dutch Resistance became active and underground newspapers thrived. Canadian troops liberated Amsterdam on 5 May 1945.

9 Mid-1960s: Provo Demonstrations

The radical Provo movement took off in the 1960s, fuelled by antagonism to the city's transport and housing policies. Demonstrations turned into rioting on 10 March 1966, the day of Princess Beatrix's wedding to German aristocrat Claus von Amsberg. The movement's popularity among the voters, however, was short-lived.

Coronation of Willem-Alexander

10 2013: Coronation of Willem-Alexander

Queen Beatrix announced her abdication in January 2013. Crown Prince Willem-Alexander was crowned the King of the Netherlands on 30 April 2013 in a grand ceremony in the Nieuwe Kerk. At 46, Willem-Alexander became the youngest monarch in Europe and the first Dutch king in 123 years.

TOP 10 HISTORIC CHARACTERS

Pieter Stuyvesant surrendering

1 Willem, Prince of Orange
"William the Silent" (1533–1584) led the Protestant rebellion against Felipe II. Willem was assassinated.

2 Willem Barentsz
This explorer (1550–1597) failed to discover the northeast passage but left behind invaluable maps.

3 Frederik Hendrik
An effective politician, William the Silent's youngest son (1584–1647) became *stadhouder* in 1625.

4 Pieter Stuyvesant
Stuyvesant (1592–1672) was Governor of the colony of Nieuw Amsterdam, later to be New York, from 1646 to 1664.

5 Abel Tasman
In search of trade routes to South America, Tasman (1603–c.1659) discovered Tasmania and New Zealand.

6 Michiel de Ruyter
This revered Dutch admiral (1607–1676) set fire to the English fleet in the Medway in 1667.

7 Jan de Witt
A leading politician during the Anglo-Dutch Wars (1625–1672), he was killed by a House of Orange mob.

8 Willem III
Willem (1650–1702) was *stadhouder* from 1672 until his promotion to King of England, Scotland and Ireland in 1689.

9 Louis Napoleon
Brother of Napoleon I, Louis (1778–1846) was King of the Netherlands between 1806 and 1810.

10 Johan Thorbecke
Liberal Prime Minister Johan Rudolf Thorbecke (1798–1872) was architect of the 1848 Constitution.

🔟 Historic Buildings

Schreierstoren, built as a defence tower in 1481, is now a café

1 Schreierstoren
MAP Q2 ▪ Prins Hendrikkade 94–5

The Schreierstoren (Tower of Tears) is one of Amsterdam's oldest buildings *(see p14)* – a surviving fragment of the medieval city wall.

2 In't Aepjen
One of two remaining wood-fronted houses in Amsterdam *(see p26)*, In't Aepjen was built in 1550 as a sailors' hostel, and is now a bar. The name means "In the monkeys"; when sailors couldn't pay, they would barter – sometimes with pet monkeys *(see p84)*.

3 Oost-Indisch Huis
MAP P4 ▪ Oude Hoogstraat 24 ▪ closed to the public

The impressive red-brick façade, with its ornate entrance and stone-dressed windows, was the height of corporate fashion. Headquarters of the once mighty Dutch East India Company (VOC), it was built in 1605, probably by Hendrick de Keyser, and is now part of Amsterdam University. The 17th-century meeting room of the VOC lords has been restored.

4 De Gooyer Windmill
MAP H4 ▪ Funenkade 5

If you are lucky, you might see the vast, streamlined sails of this 18th-century corn mill creak into motion. Built in 1725, the whole octagonal structure was painstakingly moved to its present site in 1814.

5 Pintohuis
MAP P4 ▪ Sint Antoniesbreestraat 69

Named after the Portuguese merchant Isaac de Pinto, who paid an exorbitant 30,000 guilders for it in 1651, the building boasts an Italianate façade, a Louis XIV-style chimney piece and mock-18th-century ceiling paintings. The ground floor is now a library, run by local volunteers.

Pintohuis interior

6 Trippenhuis
MAP P4 ■ Kloveniersburgwal 29

Justus Vingboons' grandiose façade with false middle windows (1662) concealed the two separate homes of the wealthy and powerful Trip brothers, Louis and Hendrick. The pair were arms dealers, hence the pair of chimneys resembling cannon and other references to weaponry in its façade.

7 West-Indisch Huis
MAP D2 ■ Haarlemmerstraat 75, (entrance: Herenmarkt 99)

The city of New York was conceived in the Dutch West India Company building, and Pieter Stuyvesant's *(see p45)* statue still surveys the courtyard. Built in 1615, its classical proportions belie its origins as a meat market.

8 Scheepvaarthuis
MAP Q2 ■ Prins Hendrikkade 108

Originally a shipping company office designed by Van der Mey, De Klerk and Kramer, this building (1916) is considered the first true example of the Amsterdam School of design and is smothered in nautical whimsy. It is now a luxury hotel.

Scheepvaarthuis detail

9 Eerste Hollandsche Verzekeringsbank
MAP L2 ■ Keizersgracht 174–6

Gerrit van Arkel's eye-catching 1905 building is a fine example of *Nieuwe Kunst*, the Dutch version of Art Nouveau. Built for an insurance company, it houses lawyers' offices and PR companies.

10 Former City Orphanage
MAP K6 ■ Prinsengracht 434–6

This sober, monumental building in Empire style is a conversion of the Almoners' Orphanage by city architect Jan de Greef. From 1829 to 2013, it housed the Court of Appeal.

TOP 10 ARCHITECTURAL FEATURES

Neck gables on Oude Turfmarkt

1 Neck Gable
Made popular by Philips Vingboons, this gable has a raised centrepiece; Oude Turfmarkt 145 is an example.

2 Triangular Gable
This simple triangular-shaped gable is seen on Het Houten Huis *(see p26)*.

3 Bell Gable
Fashionable in the late 17th and 18th centuries, bell-shaped gables can be flamboyant (Prinsengracht 126) or unadorned (Leliegracht 57).

4 Spout Gable
This plain triangular gable topped by a spout was used for warehouses, like those at Entrepotdok *(see p12)*.

5 Step Gable
Common from 1600 to 1665, this gable has steps on both sides: Huis op de Drie Grachten has three *(see p13)*.

6 Wall Plaque
Before numbering was introduced, houses were identified by illustrated plaques *(see p27)*.

7 Claw Piece
Sculptures – frequently of dolphins – were made to fill the right angles of gables. An example can be seen on Oudezijds Voorburgwal 119.

8 Mask
This type of Renaissance decoration depicts a human or animal face; it can be seen at Oudezijds Voorburgwal 57.

9 Cornices
From 1690, gables became less fashionable and decorative top mouldings came in: examples line the Herengracht.

10 Pediment Carvings
Carvings often decorate the triangular or rounded form above doorways: see the Felix Meritis Building *(see p104)*.

🔟 Dutch Artists

1 Jan van Scorel

After prolonged stays in Germany, Venice and Rome, where he studied the works of Giorgione, Michelangelo and Raphael, Jan van Scorel (1495–1562) returned to Utrecht in 1524. He introduced the techniques of the Renaissance to the Northern Netherlands; his portraits fuse Italian solidity of form with Netherlandish delicacy.

2 Rembrandt van Rijn

The greatest artist of the Dutch Golden Age (see p19).

3 Jacob van Ruisdael

Born in Haarlem, Jacob van Ruisdael (1629–1682), though not highly regarded in his own day, has come to be seen as one of the finest landscape and seascape painters of the Dutch school. His works are filled with restless skies and naturalistic details. Even calm scenes such as *The Windmill at Wijk bij Duurstede* (1670) have a dramatic sense of grandeur.

4 Johannes Vermeer

Relatively little is known about the life of this sublime Delft artist (1632–1675), who inherited his father's art-dealing business and painted purely for pleasure.

David Joris by Jan van Scorel

He gained some recognition in Holland during his lifetime, but his importance was not established until the late 19th century, and rests on fewer than 40 known works – mainly domestic interiors with figures – that are extraordinary in their handling of space, light and colour. He was married with 11 children. On his death, his wife was declared bankrupt, and his baker kept two of his paintings against unpaid bills.

5 Frans Hals

Much loved for his technique of capturing character and fleeting expression in his sitters, Frans Hals (1580–1666) brought a new realism to portraiture in the 17th century. His fine group portraits of civic guards are displayed in the Frans Hals Museum in Haarlem.

6 Vincent Van Gogh

A troubled genius (1853–1890) who left a vast body of work, despite his tragically short life (see pp20–23).

Marriage Portrait by Frans Hals

7 Willem van der Velde II

The son of a painter, Willem van der Velde the Younger (1633–1707) was the go-to painter for anything nautical, from the Dutch navy in repose to battle scenes (always of Dutch victories) and ships battered by heavy seas and cruel winds.

8 Piet Mondriaan

Piet Mondriaan (1872–1944) was born and grew up in Amersfoort, later living in Amsterdam, New York and London. A leading member of the De Stijl movement, he created an abstract style using the simplest elements: straight lines and blocks of primary colour to create harmony and balance.

The Merry Family by Jan Steen

9 Jan Steen

A prolific painter of the genre (everyday) scenes so popular in the Dutch 17th century, Jan Steen (1625–1679) was an innkeeper as well as an artist. His often bawdy narratives were packed with hidden messages (red stockings for prostitution, broken eggshells for mortality), creating allegories with a moral purpose.

10 Karel Appel

Karel Appel (1921–2006) was one of the founders of the CoBrA movement, started in 1948, which combined expressionist, abstract and surrealist influences *(see p132)*. His works display a savage, forceful directness and an almost childlike optimism. "I paint like a barbarian in a barbarous age," he said.

TOP 10 DUTCH LITERARY FIGURES

Desiderius Erasmus

1 Desiderius Erasmus
Scholar and humanist (1466–1536). Friend of Thomas More, but not of Martin Luther.

2 Hugo Grotius (or Hugo de Groot)
Statesman and philosopher (1583–1645). Author of *De Jure Belli et Pacis*, the foundation stone of international law.

3 Gerbrant Bredero
Satirical poet and playwright (1585–1618), best known for *De Spaanse Brabander*.

4 Joost van den Vondel
Important playwright and poet (1586–1679) famed for his ornate style. Author of *Gijsbrecht van Amstel*.

5 Jan Six
Poet, playwright (1618–1700) and good friend of Rembrandt, who painted his portrait.

6 Baruch Spinoza
Philosopher (1632–1677) expelled by Amsterdam's Jewish community for his secular beliefs.

7 Multatuli
Pen name of Eduard Douwes Dekker (1820–1887), whose work in colonial Java inspired his famous novel *Max Havelaar* (1860).

8 Anne Frank
Teenage victim (1929–1944) of the Holocaust. Her eloquent diary has sold in its millions.

9 Gerard Reve
Novelist (1923–2006) who wrote *The Fourth Man*.

10 Cees Nooteboom
Prolific man of letters (b.1933) whose fiction is observant and poignant, if at times experimental and elusive.

🔟 Jewish Sights

Joods Historisch Museum

1 Joods Historisch Museum

This remarkable museum represents all aspects of Judaism and the history and culture of the Jews who settled in the Netherlands and its colonies. Only a fraction of the extensive and eclectic collection of 16,000 objects is ever on show at any one time. Displays include works by Jewish artists, ceremonial items and themed exhibitions (see p82).

2 Anne Frank House

The plight of Jews like the Franks, forced into hiding by the Nazis in World War II, was brought to light by Anne's poignant diary; the house where they hid for 25 months is now a museum (see pp38–9).

3 Portuguese Synagogue

Inspired by the Temple of Solomon in Jerusalem, Elias Bouman's bulky red-brick synagogue is still the core of the small Sephardic community for whom it was built in 1675. The massive wooden barrel-vaulted ceiling is lit by more than 1,000 candles (see p82).

4 Jodenbuurt
MAP Q5

When the Jews arrived in the late 16th century, they moved into a lack-lustre area to the east of Oude Zijde, around present-day Waterlooplein. Although several synagogues, diamond factories and street markets have survived, the heart of the Jodenbuurt was destroyed by post-war redevelopment and the building of the Metro.

5 De Dokwerker
MAP Q5 ■ Jonas Daniel Meijerplein

Mari Andriessen's evocative bronze statue (1952) is a memorial to the dockers' and transport workers' strike of February 1941 over the arrest of 450 Jews for the killing of a Nazi sympathizer. The event is commemorated every 25 February.

6 Ravensbrück Memorial
MAP C6 ■ Museumplein

Remembering the women of Ravensbrück, this is one of the most disturbing of the city's Holocaust memorials. Dedicated in 1975, it incorporates a sinister soundtrack and flashing lights.

The bema and Torah ark in the Portuguese Synagogue

7 Hollandsche Schouwburg

Jewish families were rounded up at this operetta theatre before being transported to the death camps. A moving memorial and a small exhibition of memorabilia keep their memory alive *(see p129)*.

8 Verzetsmuseum Amsterdam

The Dutch Resistance Museum's brilliant displays give a vivid sense of life in an occupied country, as well as an insight into the ingenious activities of the Dutch Resistance. Exhibits include photographs, heart-rending letters thrown from deportation trains, film clips and room sets *(see p128)*.

Tuschinski Theater

9 Tuschinski Theater

This extraordinary 1921 theatre *(see p112)* was the creation of its obsessive owner, Abraham Tuschinski, a Jewish emigré who died at Auschwitz. The sumptuous interior crosses Art Deco with the Orient.

10 Nooit Meer Auschwitz

MAP R5 ■ Wertheimpark

In stark contrast to its peaceful surroundings in Wertheimpark, Jan Wolkers' 1977 Auschwitz memorial *Never More* features a slab of shattered glass. The fragments reflect a distorted view of the heavens, mirroring the damage done to humanity by the Holocaust.

TOP 10 JEWISH HISTORICAL EVENTS

Liberated Jews in 1945

1 1592 onwards
Sephardic Jews from Portugal and Spain, fleeing the Inquisition, settle in Amsterdam, attracted by the city's religious tolerance.

2 1630s
Poor Ashkenazi Jews start to arrive from eastern Europe (mainly Poland and Germany).

3 1796
Jews are given equal civil rights during Napoleon's Batavian Republic.

4 1860
Drawn to Amsterdam by its new industries and housing, Jews emigrate from Antwerp.

5 1932–1937
The Dutch Nazi Party rises under Anton Mussert; there are waves of Jewish immigration from Hitler's Germany.

6 1941
In February, nine months into German Occupation, dockworkers strike in protest at the round-up of 450 Jews.

7 1942
The deportation of the Jews to Nazi death camps begins. Many, including Anne Frank's family, go into hiding. Of the 80,000 living in pre-war Amsterdam, only 5,000 will survive the war.

8 1945
Amsterdam is liberated from Germany by Canadian troops on 5 May.

9 1947
Anne Frank's diary is published in the Netherlands *(see pp38–9)*.

10 1975
Violent protests break out against the destruction of the Jodenbuurt – the old Jewish Quarter – in the Nieuwmarkt.

🔟 Museums

⑤ Museum Willet-Holthuysen

Like the Museum Van Loon, the Willet-Holthuysen offers a fascinating glimpse inside a grand canal house – and into the lives of the wealthy merchants who lived there. Originally built in 1685, the interior is now decorated in an ornate 18th-century style. A mild sense of melancholy pervades the building (see p111).

⑥ Anne Frank House

This world-famous yet movingly simple museum is dedicated to the young diarist who hid here with her family in "the Secret Annex" from the Nazis during World War II (see pp38–9).

① Rijksmuseum
The world's greatest collection of 17th-century Dutch art, together with pieces from the Middle Ages to the 20th century, are housed in this great art museum (see pp16–19).

② Van Gogh Museum
The permanent home for hundreds of works by this troubled artist also displays work by his contemporaries (see pp20–23).

③ Amsterdam Museum
First a convent, then the city orphanage, now a wonderfully informative museum charting the history of Amsterdam and, in particular, its meteoric rise during the Golden Age (see pp30–33).

④ Museum Ons' Lieve Heer op Solder
The 17th-century domestic interiors would be fascinating in themselves, but the astonishing thing about this historic canal house is the secret Catholic church hidden on its upper floors, one of many clandestine churches built in Amsterdam after the Alteration (see pp24–5).

Anne Frank House

Modern "bathtub" extension of the Stedelijk Museum

7 Stedelijk Museum

After an extensive renovation project, the Stedelijk Museum *(see p121)* reopened to the public in 2012. A new wing designed by Benthem Crouwel Architekten has created more space for the museum's unique collection. The Stedelijk now contains 1,100 sq m (11,840 sq ft) of underground exhibition space, a sculpture hall and the futurist "bathtub" for cutting-edge exhibitions. A gift shop and a café overlook Museumplein.

8 Museum Het Rembrandthuis

Completely restored to look as it did in Rembrandt's day, this handsome red-shuttered house was the artist's home during his years of prosperity (1639–1658). Entering the rooms is a little like stepping into a painting: there are typical Dutch interiors with black-and-white tiled floors, traditional box beds, and paintings by Rembrandt's contemporaries. Perhaps the two most fascinating sights here are the recreation of his studio, and his magical etchings, of which there is a permanent exhibition that changes regularly. Many show Rembrandt's compassion for the common people, beggars and street musicians. A video about the restoration work is shown in the basement *(see p81)*.

9 Het Scheepvaartmuseum

Holding the largest collection of model ships in the world, and crammed with fascinating objects, the former naval storehouse became a museum in 1973 when the Dutch Navy vacated the building. Solid and foursquare, Daniel Stalpaert's imposing Classical-style arsenal was built for the Admiralty in 1656 during the Golden Age of Dutch maritime history. Interactive exhibits and children's activities have made the museum a much more user-friendly experience following four years of extensive renovation *(see p127)*.

Het Scheepvaartmuseum

10 Museum Van Loon

Another canal house-turned-museum, the Van Loon recreates high-society life as it was during the 18th century *(see pp36–7)*.

🔟 Churches

① Oude Kerk
The oldest and greatest of Amsterdam's churches *(see pp34–5)*.

② Nieuwe Kerk
The second parish church in Amsterdam was built after the congregation outgrew the Oude Kerk. After a fire in 1645, its oldest surviving part is the choir, dating from around 1400 *(see p41)*.

Westerkerk

③ Westerkerk
After the Alteration of 1578 *(see p25)*, the first Dutch Protestant churches to be built were the Zuiderkerk, the Noorderkerk and the Westerkerk – all designed by Hendrick de Keyser. The Westerkerk has the city's tallest tower, topped by the gaily painted imperial crown of Maximilian of Austria *(see p95)*.

④ Zuiderkerk
The splendid spire, with its columns, clocks, pinnacles and onion dome, was much admired by Sir Christopher Wren, and is still a prominent city landmark, with superb views over the city from the tower *(see p85)*. The Zuiderkerk ceased to function as a church in 1929.

⑤ De Krijtberg
MAP M5 ▪ Singel 448
▪ Open noon–1:15pm & 5–6:15pm Mon & Fri, noon–6:15pm Tue–Thu & Sat, 9am–6:30pm Sun ▪ English mass 5:15pm Sat ▪ www.krijtberg.nl

Like many Catholic churches in the city, De Krijtberg (Chalk Mountain) is known by its nickname rather than its official name, Franciscus Xaveriuskerk (after St Francis Xavier, a founding Jesuit monk); designed in 1884 by Alfred Tepe, it replaced a clandestine Jesuit chapel *(see p25)*. It has an elegant, twin-steepled Neo-Gothic façade and an ornate interior that stands in marked contrast to the austerity of the city's Protestant churches.

⑥ Noorderkerk
MAP D2 ▪ Noordermarkt 48
▪ Open Jul & Aug: 10:30am–12:30pm Sat; Sep–Jun: 10:30am–12:30pm Mon & Sat (regular afternoon concerts on Sat) ▪ www.noorderkerk.org

Hendrick de Keyser's last church, begun a year before he died in 1621 (its completion was supervised by his son Pieter), is quite different in style from the Zuiderkerk and Westerkerk. Built for the poor of the Jordaan, it is an austere brick building with only the shortest of spires. Designed on a Greek Cross plan, it has a central pulpit and four hipped roofs.

Noorderkerk

7 Engelse Kerk

In the middle of the Begijnhof, the pretty English Reformed Church got its name from the English (and Scottish) Presbyterians who worshipped there after it was requisitioned in 1578. Prior to the Alteration, it was used by the Beguines (a Catholic sisterhood) who lived in the Begijnhof. In fact, there has been a church on this site since the end of the 14th century (see p26).

8 Mozes en Aäronkerk

MAP Q5 ■ Waterlooplein 205

Here, the nickname comes from two gablestones depicting Moses and Aäron on the house fronts that hid a clandestine church within. These are now set into the rear wall. The hidden church was replaced in 1841 by the present Neo-Classical building, its towers inspired by St Sulpice in Paris.

9 Waalse Kerk

MAP P4 ■ Walenpleintje 159

This church – founded in 1409 – is all that is left of the convent of St Paul. Its name means Walloon Church, a reference to Wallonia (now Belgium), from where Huguenots fled the Catholic terror. In 1586, they were given use of the Waalse Kerk so that they could continue their worship in French. The church's first organ, built in 1680, needed so much maintenance that it was replaced with a brand new instrument, which master organ builder Christian Müller finished in 1734. Today, Waalse Kerk is also a beautiful and popular concert venue, primarily for performances of classical music.

Neo-Baroque St Nicolaasbasiliek

10 St Nicolaasbasiliek

MAP Q1 ■ Prins Hendrikkade 73 ■ Open noon–3pm Mon and Sat, 11am–4pm Tue–Fri ■ Mass 12:30pm Mon–Sat, 10.30am, 1pm, 5pm Sun; in English on Tue ■ www.nicolaas-parochie.nl

Dedicated to the patron saint of seafarers, the church was commissioned by the congregation of Ons' Lieve Heer op Solder (see pp24–5). A C Bleys, the architect, came up with a Neo-Baroque building with its stunning stained glass.

🔟 Walks and Cycle Rides

Canal houses and colourful houseboats along Prinsengracht

① Prinsengracht
At 3 km (2 miles), the outermost canal of the Grachtengordel *(see p15)* makes a very pleasant, fairly car-free walk or cycle ride, with plenty of cafés at which to rest along the way.

② Shopping Walk
Beginning at Noordermarkt *(see p96)*, take Prinsengracht to the Negen Straatjes *(see p103)* with its quirky shops. Have a look at De Looier antiques market in Elandsgracht before heading down Lijnbaansgracht to Leidseplein. Turn up Leidsestraat for its many designer stores and boutiques, then on to Bloemenmarkt *(see p112)*, ending at De Bijenkorf on Damrak *(see p73)*.

③ Nightlife Walk
Start at the entertainment hub, Leidseplein *(see p105)*, before moving to the bright lights around Rembrandtplein *(see p111)*. Wind down at the junction of Reguliersgracht with Herengracht, where you can see no fewer than 15 romantically lit bridges. Continue to Amstelkerk, finishing in Utrechtsestraat, with its many appealing cafés *(see p114)* and restaurants *(see p115)*.

④ Herengracht
The most fascinating of the Grachtengordel *(see pp12–15)*, the Herengracht is lined with beautiful buildings, such as Bartolotti House (Nos. 170–172), the Cromhouthuis *(see p103)* and the mansions of the Golden Bend *(see p12)*.

⑤ Around Oudeschans
From Centraal Station, discover a quiet part of the old city by taking Binnenkant, lined with fine houses, and then, passing Montelbaanstoren, walk along Oudeschans to reach the Rembrandthuis *(see p81)*. Pause for refreshment at De Sluyswacht, the crooked café on the bridge *(see p84)*, before exploring the old Jewish quarter, Jodenbuurt *(see p50)*, or continuing to lively Nieuwmarkt *(see p81)*.

⑥ To Ouderkerk aan de Amstel
For a tranquil cycle ride, follow the Amstel from the city centre (start near Blauwbrug) to Ouderkerk aan de Amstel *(see p132)*. The route passes Amstelpark and the De Rieker windmill before entering attractive countryside. The journey is about a 20-km (12-mile) round trip.

7 Plantage

With its distinguished villas, tree-lined streets, parks and gardens, Plantage *(see pp126–9)* is a calm district to explore by bike (with the exception of busy thoroughfare Plantage Middenlaan).

8 Western Islands

Perhaps the most peaceful part of Amsterdam in which to walk or cycle lies to the northwest of Centraal Station. The islands of Prinseneiland, Bickerseiland and Realeneiland, together known as the Western Islands, have a remote, bracing quality, with well-worn boatyards and white drawbridges, as well as modern housing *(see p97)*.

9 Amsterdamse Bos

This attractive wooded park south of the city is ideal for cyclists, thanks to 48 km (30 miles) of cycle path; those on foot have no less than 160 km (100 miles) of footpath to stroll along. Perfect for a family picnic outing *(see p131)*.

Bridge over Brouwersgracht, Jordaan

10 Jordaan

Start at Westerkerk *(see p95)*, perhaps climbing its tower for a bird's-eye view of the area. Work your way north to picturesque Brouwersgracht *(see p96)*.

TOP 10 TIPS FOR CYCLING IN AMSTERDAM

Cyclists in Amsterdam

1 Stick to the Rules
Don't copy the locals, who jump red lights and ride against the traffic flow.

2 Stay in the Cycle Lanes
Amsterdam has an excellent integrated network of *fietspaden* (cycle lanes), with white lines, cycle signs and dedicated traffic lights.

3 Cross Tramlines with Care
If you have to, cross tramlines at a right angle to avoid your front wheel getting stuck.

4 Avoid Trams
They are bigger than you, and can't be steered; listen for their rattle and stay well clear of the lines.

5 Watch for Pedestrians
It's usually tourists who mistakenly walk in cycle lanes; keep an eye out for parked cars, too.

6 Give Priority
Watch out for trams as they get priority over all other traffic.

7 Dismount at Busy Junctions
Unless you are really confident, it's better to negotiate these on foot.

8 Don't Cycle Two-Abreast
It's only allowed if you are not obstructing the traffic; otherwise, stay in single file.

9 Use Lights
By law, you must turn your lights on after dusk – you must also have reflector bands on both wheels. Ensure hire bicycles come with both.

10 Lock Your Bike
Bicycle theft is rife. Make sure that you always lock both front wheel and frame to an immovable object.

TOP 10 Off The Beaten Track

Peaceful Groenburgwal with Zuiderkerk's spire in the distance

1 Groenburgwal
MAP P5 ▪ **Groenburgwal**

Tucked away near the university, Groenburgwal is perhaps Amsterdam's prettiest canal, a narrow sliver of water lined by mature trees and handsome houses, with the spire of the Zuiderkerk in the middle distance. It's best viewed from the sweet little swing bridge on Staalstraat.

2 Westerpark
MAP C1 ▪ **Haarlemmerweg**

Revamped and re-landscaped, the Westerpark is a pleasant slice of greenery sandwiched between the Haarlemervaart canal and a railway embankment. Waterfowl swim around the park's ponds, and joggers and walkers share the footpaths The 19th-century gasworks next door to the park – the Westergasfabriek – is now a cultural centre hosting arts and entertainment events.

3 Hofje van Brienen
MAP D2 ▪ **Prinsengracht 89–133** ▪ **Open 6am–6pm Mon–Fri, 6am–2pm Sat**

Behind a modest little door on the Prinsengracht, the Hofje van Brienen is a trim, brown-brick courtyard complex built as an almshouse in 1804 on the site of what was once a brewery. For decades it provided sheltered lodgings for the poor and needy and, although it's more upmarket today, it remains a tranquil spot.

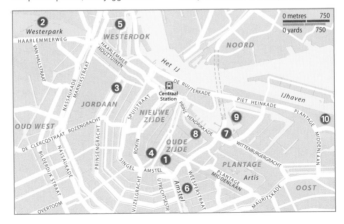

4 Oudemanhuispoort
MAP N4 ■ Oudemanhuispoort, off Kloveniersburgwal ■ Book stalls: open 9am–5pm, Mon–Sat

Once an almshouse complex for elderly men, the Oudemanhuispoort is now no more than a covered passageway off Kloveniersburgwal. It has, however, been re-purposed to accommodate a series of second-hand bookstalls, a suitable location as the university is close by.

5 Zandhoek
MAP D1 ■ Zandhoek

In a pretty location on the Western Islands, Zandhoek is an appealing little street with a string of old sea captains' houses that once had uninterrupted views over the harbour. The wall plaque on No. 14 (De Gouden Reael) sports a golden coin after which the house is named.

Zandhoek

6 Nieuwe Keizersgracht 58
MAP Q6 ■ Nieuwe Keizersgracht

It was here at luxurious No. 58, with its Neo-Classical double doorway, that the Judenrat (the Jewish Council through which the Germans managed the ghetto) met from 1940 onwards. There's no plaque outside as the role of the Judenrat is still controversial.

7 Arcam
MAP G3 ■ Prins Hendrikkade 600 ■ 020 620 4878 ■ Open Tue–Sun 1–5pm ■ www.arcam.nl/en

Inhabiting a striking modern building designed by René van

Van Zuuk's striking Arcam building

Zuuk, Arcam (Amsterdam's Centre for Architecture) has a small display area devoted to temporary exhibitions on the city and its buildings. Arcam also produces several excellent architectural guides (in English) and consults on planning for new city developments.

8 Binnenkant
MAP Q3 ■ Binnenkant

Well off the tourist-beaten track, this appealing side canal is lined with houseboats and fine old merchants' houses. Well-placed benches at the junction with Kalkmarkt overlook a charming stretch of the Oudeschans canal, the site of Amsterdam's first shipyards.

9 Marine Terrein Amsterdam
MAP G3 ■ Kattenburgerstraat

Occupied by the Dutch Royal Navy for centuries, this corner of the city has been open to the public since 2011. The area offers relatively quiet surroundings that include waterside lawns, which are perfect for picnics.

10 Lloyd Hotel
Oostelijke Handelskade 34 ■ 020 561 3607 ■ www.lloydhotel.com

Opened in 1921, the Lloyd Hotel (see p145) was built beside the IJhaven dock for the transit passengers of a major shipping company. It subsequently saw service as a refugee centre and a detention centre. An interesting exhibition inside the hotel explores its turbulent past.

🔟 Children's Attractions

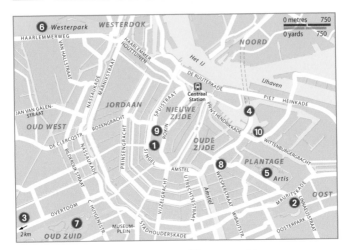

① The Little Orphanage
Visitors to The Little Orphanage children's exhibition at the Amsterdam Museum *(see pp30–33)* can experience what life was like in a 17th-century orphanage. Children are sent on engaging quests to find hidden animals, or discover more about an orphan boy called Jurriaan.

② Tropenmuseum
Learn about the cultural diversity of Africa, or pore over Dutch colonial history in this museum dedicated to ethnography and contemporary art. Tropenmuseum Junior, the "hands-on" museum for children aged 6 to 13, is open by appointment, with tours in Dutch, or English tours by special request *(see p127)*.

Tropenmuseum

③ Tram Rides
Electrische Museumtramlijn: Haarlemmermeerstation, Amstelveenseweg 264 ▪ 020 673 7538 ▪ Trams depart Easter–Oct: 11am–5pm Sun ▪ Adm ▪ www.museum tramlijn.org

Go to Haarlemmermeer railway station and then take a 20-minute ride in an old-fashioned tram with wooden seats, clanging bell and friendly conductor to Amsterdamse Bos, where you will find pancakes, peacocks, and plenty of leg-stretching space.

④ NEMO
It's worth going to the science and technology centre for the building alone – dubbed "Titanic" – and for the superb views you can get from the top deck. Inside, enquiring minds will be kept alert with experiments and demonstrations *(see pp128–9)*.

⑤ Artis Royal Zoo
Children love this action-packed zoo, where they can pat the animals in the children's farm, brave

Relaxing in Westerpark

the steamy reptile house, see stars in the planetarium and marvel at the fish in the aquarium (see p127).

6 Westerpark

Children's farm: 023 682 2193 Open 9am–5pm Tue–Sun ▪ Woeste Westen: open 11am–6pm Wed, Sat–Sun, 1–6pm Mon, Tue, Thu & Fri ▪ www.woestewesten.nl

With entertainment for kids and parents alike, this cultural park has an arts complex, Sunday markets, outdoor wading pool, playgrounds, children's farm, Het Woeste Westen natural adventure park, and plenty of cafés to boot.

7 Vondelpark

Together with the smaller Westerpark, this is the perfect place to go with kids on a summer's day. It has a paddling pool, playgrounds, Kinderkookkafé (Kids Café) and a children's Art Club on Wednesday afternoons (at the Groot Melkhuis café) (see p121).

8 TunFun

MAP Q5 ▪ Mr Visserplein 7 ▪ 020 689 4300 ▪ Open 10am–6pm daily ▪ Closed 1 Jan, 27 Apr ▪ Adm ▪ www.tunfun.nl

This vast indoor adventure playground occupies a disused underpass. Parents can sit back and relax as pre-teens run wild in the warren of tunnels, slides and trampolines, while toddlers romp in their own special area.

9 Madame Tussauds Amsterdam

Surprising, educational and, at times, emotional encounters with superheroes and film stars are to be had here (see pp40–41). There is a great view across Dam Square from the round window, too.

10 East Indiaman Amsterdam

A splendid replica of a Dutch East India Company cargo ship that sank on its maiden voyage in 1749. Watch the sailors hoisting cargo and swabbing decks. Built in 1991, it is moored outside Het Scheepvaartmuseum (see p127).

East Indiaman *Amsterdam*, moored outside Het Scheepvaartmuseum

🔟 Performing Arts Venues

Live performance at AFAS Live

1 AFAS Live
ArenA Boulevard 590 ▪ 0900 687 4242 ▪ www.afaslive.nl

Amsterdam's third-biggest live music venue (the ArenA next door, home to Ajax football team, is the biggest). Designed especially for amplified music, it offers world-class acoustics and a great ambience during concerts.

2 Boom Chicago
MAP J3 ▪ Rozentheater, Rozengracht 117 ▪ 020 217 0400 ▪ www.boomchicago.nl

On a daily basis, this US comedy crew puts on satirical shows whose targets are anything from Dutch "quirks" to topical news issues. The beer, served in huge pitchers, is a welcome respite from the tiny frothy-headed *pilsjes*. Starwatchers note: Burt Reynolds once popped in.

3 Stadsschouwburg
MAP C5 ▪ Leidseplein 26 ▪ 020 624 2311 ▪ www.ssba.nl, www.hollandfestival.nl

This Neo-Renaissance building – both of whose precursors burned down – houses the city's municipal theatre. Local theatre groups, such as Toneelgroep Amsterdam, as well as visiting companies tread the boards here. The venue also hosts dance performances, most notably the annual Julidans (July Dance) Festival.

4 Concertgebouw
The *crème de la crème* of international musicians and conductors appear at this palatial classical music venue *(see p122)*. Audrey Hepburn had a season ticket when she lived in Amsterdam, and it's not hard to understand why. Don't miss the free lunchtime concerts on Wednesdays.

5 Koninklijk Theater Carré
Originally built as a circus theatre in 1894, this impressive landmark on the banks of the Amstel still hosts circus troupes, along with anything from opera to ballet, magicians to music *(see p128)*. Nothing beats sipping champagne on the balcony overlooking the river on a warm evening.

Circus performer at Carré

6 Nationale Opera & Ballet
The Dutch royals regularly pop in to catch shows at this comfortable modern theatre, which is home to the Netherlands Opera and Ballet companies and has the largest auditorium in the country *(see p83)*. Tickets for shows – particularly opera – can sell out months in advance, so it's best to book before you travel. Inspired programming, including the revival of little-known

operas and brand new opera performances makes this an exciting venue for contemporary culture vultures.

7 Melkweg

This multimedia centre (the Milky Way) occupies a former dairy behind the Stadsschouwburg. Opened in 1970, the venue offers a wide range of entertainment including live music, film, theatre and dance (see p109).

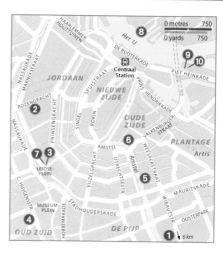

8 Tolhuistuin

MAP F1

■ Buiksloterweg 5C

■ 020 763 0650 ■ www.tolhuistuin.nl

The former Shell staff canteen is now a cultural hotspot, hosting a wide variety of music, dance, art exhibitions and literary events. There's a fine café and acoustic performances take place in the garden in summer.

9 Bimhuis

MAP G2 ■ Piet Heinkade 3

■ 020 788 2188 ■ www.bimhuis.nl

Sticking out of the Muziekgebouw aan 't IJ like a Siamese twin, the remarkable Bimhuis is a popular stage for jazz and improvised music. New talent rubs shoulders with established musicians here and there are plenty of opportunities to hear electronic and world music.

10 Muziekgebouw aan 't IJ

MAP G2 ■ Piet Heinkade 1

■ 020 788 2000 ■ www.muziekge bouw.nl

Amsterdam's spectacular concert hall for the 21st century opened in 2005. It occupies a unique position on a peninsula on the IJ, which gives it magnificent views. As well as a 735-seat main auditorium there is a smaller 125-seat hall, foyer decks overlooking the IJ and a café restaurant, the Zouthaven, with a waterfront terrace. The venue's impressive programme concentrates mainly on contemporary works.

Striking modern building of the Muziekgebouw aan 't IJ and Bimhuis

🔟 Restaurants

1 Supperclub

Dine while you relax on large white comfy beds, and enjoy a night's sensory experience with your meal (see p90). Avant-garde performance, live DJs, excellent cocktails and innovative art and entertainment are served up alongside five courses from a kitchen not afraid to experiment. Supperclub cruise on the IJ takes the experience onto the water. There is also a HOPPA Beercafé and Speakeasy Bar on site.

Trendy interior of Supperclub

2 Van Vlaanderen

MAP E5 ■ Weteringschans 175
■ 020 622 8292 ■ €€€

The decor may be plain, but the dishes are rich and elaborate at this gourmands' paradise, for years known only to insiders until the restaurant acquired a number-one Zagat rating. Expect to feast on goose-liver, suckling pig, pigeon breasts, sweetbreads and other delightfully wicked fare.

3 De Hallen

MAP B4 ■ Bellamyplein 18
■ 020 705 8164 ■ €€

Think epicurean gourmet meets food court in this refurbished, early 20th-century tram depot. Perfect for when you can't decide on where to eat, it is lined with a wide choice of superb food stalls and seating areas. It also has an excellent grill restaurant, Meat West, a meat-eater's paradise.

4 Daalder Eten & Drinken

MAP D2 ■ Lindengracht 90
■ 020 624 8864 ■ €€€

What seems like a traditional bruin café (see p67) is in fact a sophisticated restaurant, serving exquisite food in a relaxed, atmosphere. A favourite of locals and those looking to escape the more touristy commercialized city centre.

5 Bridges Restaurant

MAP N4 ■ Oudezijds Voorburgwal 197 ■ 020 555 3560
■ www.bridgesrestaurant.nl ■ €€€

The sleek, modern look of the Grand Hotel's restaurant was inspired by Karl Appel's huge 1949 mural, *Asking Children*, which crowns the restaurant's entrance. Chef Aurélien Poirot, specializing in seafood accompanied by seasonal, locally sourced, organic vegetables, delivers nothing but the finest.

6 Hemelse Modder

MAP Q3 ■ Oude Waal 11
■ 020 624 3203 ■ €€€

Reservations are essential at this friendly, off-the-beaten-track restaurant, renowned for its imaginative French- and Italian-influenced international cuisine and choice wine list. Besides the attentive service, its best kept secret is its charming alleyway terrace. Fixed-price menus and vegetarian options available. Definitely worth sniffing out.

7 Tujuh Maret

MAP E5 ■ Utrechtsestraat 73
■ 020 427 9865 ■ €€

Treating yourself to an Indonesian rijsttafel (rice table) is an absolute must in Amsterdam – and this one is outstanding. Enjoy a feast of 18 deliciously spicy dishes, from mild to explosively chilli-filled, flavoured with coconut and ginger, peanuts and lemongrass, all served with heaped mounds of rice. This is a great option for dining in a group.

⑧ Mamouche
MAP D6 ▪ Quellijnstraat 104
▪ 020 670 0736 ▪ €€€

Join a super-fashionable crowd to experience the very best of Moroccan and French cuisine. Familiar dishes like lamb tagine and couscous share the menu alongside the chef's much more elaborate and exotic creations, such as the delicious stewed rabbit and sesame with baked apricots and cinnamon seeds.

⑨ De Kas
Kamerlingh Onneslaan 3
▪ 020 462 4562 ▪ Closed Sun
▪ www.restaurantdekas.nl ▪ €€€

You cannot get fresher or more locally sourced food than at this stunning greenhouse restaurant. Under its high glass ceiling, diners nestle among organic herbs and vegetables grown by Michelin-starred chef (and owner) Gert Jan Hageman. The menu, prepared by head chef Bas Wiegel, is a five-course menu that changes with the seasons. Worth the trip.

Middle Eastern-themed Bazar

⑩ Bazar
A lofty, former synagogue provides a stunning home for this fantastic Eastern-influenced restaurant. Decorated with colourful tables and lanterns, Bazar is a great place to dine after a day browsing the myriad market stalls. Expect delicious North African, Iranian and Middle Eastern delights *(see p115)*.

TOP 10 DUTCH FOODS

Patat with mayonnaise

1 Patat
Originating in Belgium, Dutch *patat* (chips) are typically eaten with a large dollop of mayonnaise.

2 Maatjes Haring
Fresh soused herring, with chopped onion or gherkin, is sold as a snack from street stalls. Best in June, when the *nieuwe* (new season's) herrings appear.

3 Gerookte Paling
Paling (smoked eel) comes from the IJsselmeer, and is served with white toast and a squeeze of lemon.

4 Kaas
The Dutch consume a staggering 14 kg (31 lb) of cheese per person each year. Gouda and Edam are the best known.

5 Bitterballen
These deep-fried meatballs have a crunchy exterior and a hot soft meat filling. Best with mustard and a beer.

6 Hutspot
Hutspot (meaning hotchpotch) is a stew of braised beef and potatoes mashed with carrots.

7 Erwtensoep
A pea soup some foreigners find hard to love, with a consistency akin to wallpaper paste. Served with rye bread.

8 Rijsttafel
Indonesian cuisine is popular in the form of *rijsttafel* (rice table), as many as 25 little dishes of meat, vegetables and sauces around a shared bowl of rice or noodles.

9 Appelgebak
The classic apple pie, with a large dollop of *slagroom* (whipped cream).

10 Pannenkoeken
Dutch pancakes are often topped with syrup called *stroop*. The mini versions are called *Poffertjes*.

For a key to restaurant price ranges see p84

🔟 Cafés

Canal-side terrace at De Jaren

1 De Jaren

Wood, air, glass and light seem the building elements of this spacious, multi-levelled grand café. Have a leisurely leaf through international newspapers at the reading table, pile up your plate at the salad bar, or sun yourself beside the canal on one of the best terraces in town (see p90).

2 Royal Café De Kroon

MAP N6 ■ Rembrandtplein 17 ■ 020 625 2011 ■ www.dekroon.nl ■ €€€

Elegant with an eclectic touch, the Royal Café De Kroon was named for the coronation of Queen Wilhelmina in 1898. The latest incarnation includes deep chairs and a large balcony. The restaurant serves some of the finest, good-value Dutch and International cuisine in town. Enjoy cocktails and salsa dancing on Wednesdays and Sundays. Thursday, Friday and Saturday are DJ nights.

3 Het Blauwe Theehuis

"The Blue Teahouse" (see p125) in the middle of the Vondelpark is a 1930s architectural treasure, a trendy night spot and a great terrace café all in one. Snack on well-filled sandwiches under the trees, dine in the upstairs restaurant or pick up a coffee on your walk through the park.

4 De Bakkerswinkel

MAP P2 ■ Warmoesstraat 69; 020 489 8000 ■ Polonceaukade 1 (Westerpark); 020 688 0632 ■ www.debakkerswinkel.com ■ €

Refined cream teas, delicate sandwiches, scrumptious cakes and mouthwatering quiches, all baked on the premises, are served at this bakery in the city centre and in the Westergasfabriek west of the centre

5 Greenwoods

Take a break from sightseeing in this English-style tearoom with a charming atmosphere. Hearty all-day breakfasts, dainty high tea complete with cream cakes, and a top notch selection of hot drinks make Greenwoods a popular hangout (see p90).

Greenwoods, decorated as an English-style tearoom

6 Walem

Sip a champagne cocktail on the canal-side terrace, or indoors with the fashionable crowd at one of Amsterdam's most popular cafés (see p106). Piles of magazines and a number of intriguing artworks help while away the time.

7 De Taart van M'n Tante
MAP D6 ■ Ferdinand Bolstraat 10 ■ 020 776 4600 ■ €

"My Aunt's Cake" is the campest tearoom in town and is run by couture cake creators who supply Amsterdam's elite, including the mayor and the Dutch royal family.

8 Pacific Parc
Polonceaukade 23 ■ 020 488 7778 ■ €€

In a vast industrial building on the grounds of a former gas works, this café has Wi-Fi, an open fire in winter and canal-side terrace in summer.

1e Klas

9 1e Klas
MAP P1 ■ Platform 2b, Amsterdam Centraal Station, Stationsplein ■ 020 625 0131 ■ €€

Nominated in 2015 as one of Europe's top station restaurants, this unique venue in a 19th-century former first-class waiting room with an ornate ceiling and panelled walls transports you back in time.

10 Tis Fris
MAP P4 ■ St Antoniesbreestraat 142 ■ 020 622 0472 ■ €

A few steps from the Waterlooplein Flea Market (see p73), this light and spacious split-level café serves healthy quiches, salads and soups as well as alcohol.

TOP 10 TYPES OF CAFÉ

An eetcafé

1 Eetcafé
Eetcafé means, unsurprisingly, "eat café", and eat is exactly what you do in one. Good cooking at a little below restaurant prices.

2 Grand Café
Always grand in size, sometimes these cafés are grand in style too.

3 Bruin Café
Snug and old-fashioned, these brown cafés (so called because of the once nicotine-stained walls) are the perfect places for beer and gossip.

4 Hip Hangouts
Some cafés flash their designer credentials and attract a suitably hip and trendy crowd.

5 Music Cafés
Live music or top DJs make these a good starting point for an evening of clubbing (see pp70–71).

6 Games Cafés
Devotees of billiards, chess, darts or board games will find entire cafés given over to single pursuits.

7 Coffee & Cake
Sometimes there's no alcohol at all, just tea, coffee and more calories than you'd care to mention.

8 Nachtcafés
When all else is closed, these night cafés open their doors through the wee hours, though tread carefully – some may be a little seedy.

9 Gay Cafés
From the stylish to the sweaty, the city's famous gay cafés cater to all tastes.

10 "Coffeeshops"
Here, intoxicants take a different form, and smoking rather than drinking is the predominant activity.

🔟 Bars

3 The Minds
MAP M4
- Spuistraat 245
- 020 623 6784
- www.theminds.nl

An old-school punk bar, with combat boots and battered skateboards hanging from the rafters, The Minds is different from the usual trendy club scene in the city. It has good beer on tap, plenty of loud music and a pool table, if you think you're up to competing with the locals.

4 Prik
MAP M2
- Spuistraat 109
- 020 320 0002
- www.prikamsterdam.nl

While the name of this extremely popular, award-winning gay bar may sound rude, it's actually Dutch for "carbonation", with a nod to their signature drink – Prosecco on tap. "Spicy mango" is a favoured cocktail with tourists and locals alike (though Prik remains essentially Dutch). Monday nights bring cheap pints, on Tuesdays it's discounted gin and tonics, and on Friday and Saturday evenings, DJs pump commercial house and pop music throughout the hip rainbow-neon, dimly-lit interior.

1 De Pieper
MAP K6 - Prinsengracht 424
- 020 626 4775

This easygoing, neighbourhood brown café, just a block away from busy Leidseplein, has an especially convivial atmosphere and a pleasant location. A laid-back sort of place, with boho furniture and ancient wooden tables, it has a mini-terrace beside the canal, a good range of draft beers and a fantastic selection of liqueurs.

De Pieper

2 Brouwerij 't IJ
MAP H4 - Funenkade 7
- 020 261 9801 - Open 2–8pm daily
- www.brouwerijhetij.nl

Adjacent to an 1814 windmill and within a former bathhouse, this micro-brewery produces excellent beer. Tours of the brewery are at 4pm (in Dutch) and 4:30pm (in English) every Friday, Saturday and Sunday. Drinks can be enjoyed at the tasting house and sunny terrace until 8pm.

Prik, one of the city's popular gay bars

XtraCold, a unique experience on Amsterdam's bar scene

⑤ XtraCold
MAP P6 ■ Amstel 194–6
■ 020 320 5700 ■ www.xtracold.com

For polar conditions beyond an Amsterdam winter, XtraCold offers a 4D experience (3D film with live effects, like the wind whipping through your hair) at –10 degrees Celsius. The bar requires pre-booking online, and around €20 buys you 45 minutes in the all-ice environment, with thermals, gloves, 3D glasses, and three drinks. Recover afterwards in the warm lounge bar with some tapas and cocktails.

⑥ Barney's Uptown
MAP D2 ■ Haarlemmerstraat 105 ■ 020 427 9469 ■ www.barneys amsterdam.com

Classy Barney's Uptown, part of the Barney's coffeeshop chain, boasts a good range of beers and spectacular cocktails. The smoker-friendly bar has half-price wine, and cocktails are available on Ladies' Night on Thursdays after 7pm.

⑦ Getto
Getto is a welcome relief to the screaming neon of the Red Light District. The owners claim it is an "attitude free zone", resulting in a very mixed clientele. Liberating and friendly, with a simple, home-style menu served every evening (see p90).

⑧ Freddy's Bar
MAP N5 ■ De L'Europe, Nieuwe Doelenstraat 2–14 ■ 020 531 1707

A favourite haunt of the late Alfred "Freddy" Heineken, Freddy's Bar attracts the A-list set who flock to its leather banquettes to savour tasty cocktails, gourmet nibbles and a jazz pianist.

⑨ Café De Koe
MAP K6 ■ Marnixstraat 381
■ 020 625 4482 ■ www.cafedekoe.nl

Downstairs, people are tucking into good, basic food; upstairs, they're shoulder to shoulder around the bar. Order a beer and you're instantly part of a no-nonsense neighbourhood bar atmosphere, with just a touch of merry mayhem, and everyone aiming headlong at a good night out.

Wijnand Fockink

⑩ Wijnand Fockink
Proeflokalen, the "tasting houses" of local distilleries, were once places to knock back a quick *jenever* (Dutch gin). Crooked and cosy, with wooden barrels lining the walls, this one dates back to the 17th century (see p84).

🔟 Clubs

The interior of Escape, one of Amsterdam's best clubs

① Escape
MAP N6 ■ Rembrandtplein 11–15 ■ 020 622 1111 ■ www.escape.nl
One of Amsterdam's biggest and most exciting clubs, which can hold up to 1,300 people, has a huge dance floor, hi-tech lighting and, as you would expect, a stunning sound system. At weekends, it attracts a big out-of-town crowd.

② Westerunie
MAP B1 ■ Klönneplein 4 ■ 020 684 8496 ■ www.westerunie.nl
Situated just west of the Jordaan, the Westerunie is housed in a cavernous, industrial space that was once part of a huge gasworks. Popular for its central location, the venue hosts large-scale techno, acid, and house nights with the occasional addition of latin and disco music.

③ A'DAM Toren
MAP F1 ■ Overhoeksplein 1 ■ www.adamtoren.nl
Sitting on the harbour directly behind Centraal Station, the old Shell Tower has been transformed into A'DAM Toren with two trendy nightclubs. Madam on the 20th floor is a restaurant-bar by day and a nightclub after dark, with panoramic views. In the basement is Shelter, a cavernous club with an industrial-chic interior.

④ Melkweg
This large, rambling multi-media centre housed in an old milk factory just off Leidseplein, is one of the country's top venues for live bands. It offers everything: club nights, the hottest DJs, after parties, avant-garde theatre, art-house films, a gallery and eatery, all happily coexisting under one roof (see p63). Admission fee varies.

⑤ Jimmy Woo
MAP K6 ■ Korte Leidsedwarsstraat 18 ■ 020 626 3150 ■ www.jimmywoo.com
With its opulent interior, state-of-the-art sound system, superb lighting and celebrity clientele, Jimmy Woo is arguably Amsterdam's most glamorous club.

Jimmy Woo

6 Sugar Factory
MAP K6 ■ Lijnbaansgracht 238
■ 020 627 0008 ■ www.sugarfactory.nl

Whether it's avant-garde performances, sultry jazz or German
electro nights, this club by the
Leidseplein never fails to deliver
an impressive programme.

7 Club Nyx
MAP M6 ■ Reguliersdwars-
straat 42 ■ Closed Sun–Wed
■ www.clubnyx.nl

Whether you prefer it gay, straight,
camp, burlesque or just want to
hit the dance floor, Nyx has it all
in abundance. Named after the
Greek goddess of the night, Nyx
has three floors, each offering a
different style of music, DJs galore
and an international line-up of artists.

8 AIR
MAP P6 ■ Amstelstraat 16
■ 020 820 0670 ■ Closed Mon–Wed
■ www.air.nl

AIR maintains an intimate
atmosphere thanks to its flexible
layout. The club boasts state-of-the-
art sound and visual systems, and
offers a diverse programme for
various tastes.

9 Paradiso
Formerly a church, now
predominantly a live music venue,
Paradiso features DJs after the

Paradiso

bands have been on – with an
emphasis on alternative music.
The programming for parties can
be erratic – anything from Moroccan
dance nights to cinema-club
evenings (see p109).

10 The Winston Kingdom
MAP N3 ■ Warmoesstraat 131
■ 020 623 1380 ■ www.winston.nl

Eclectic and inspired programming
give this small, Rococo-style venue
an edge on the city's other clubs.
One of the best nights is "Cheeky
Mondays", which is perfect for an
indulgent start to the week. The
club rocks to a drum 'n' bass beat
until 4am, as well as having live
music (mostly rock 'n' roll) four
nights a week.

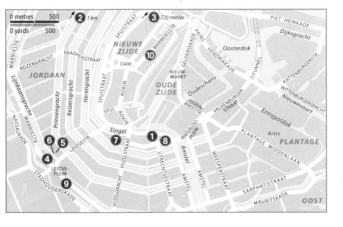

🔟 Shops and Markets

Albert Cuypmarkt

derisively dubbed "post office Gothic" by its critics – was designed by Cornelis Hendrik Peters (1874–1932) to house Amsterdam's head post office. Now a pricey shopping mall with several cafés and 40 diverse stores located over its four floors.

1 Albert Cuypmarkt
Amsterdam's largest general market runs all the way down this long street in the Pijp area, touting everything from fresh fish to footwear. Come here for fabrics, fish and seafood and odds and ends (see p111).

2 Albert Heijn
Various branches
Albert Heijn is a rather upmarket supermarket chain – there's at least one in each area of town. A little pricey, but the selection is wide, the aisles are well-stocked, and they're open late: unusually, several centrally located branches stay open until 10pm.

3 Magna Plaza
MAP M3 ■ **Nieuwezijds Voorburgwal 182**
Built between 1895 and 1899, this magnificent building – once

4 HEMA
Various branches
This ubiquitous, cheap and cheerful department store chain started life in 1926 and has become something of a Dutch institution. The store offers affordable designer products, practical clothing, stationery, kitchen equipment and food products. It also stocks its own brand of items.

Bloemenmarkt

5 Bloemenmarkt
Amsterdam's famous floating flower market – the stalls still float, but now they are permanent (see p112).

6 Boerenmarkt
MAP D2
■ **Noordermarkt**
Amsterdam's organic Saturday "farmers' market" is a treat rather than a routine shopping trip. Cruise the stalls to the accompaniment of some fine busking and sample free goats' cheese and other goodies – plus freshly baked bread, flowers and a fabulous mushroom selection.

Magna Plaza

De Bijenkorf
MAP N3 ■ Dam 1

Named "The Beehive" (which just about sums it up if you're here at the weekend), Amsterdam's prestigious department store caters for everyone from children to clubbers. Often described as the Dutch Harrods, De Bijenkorf's prices ensure that it's only the well-monied who tend to part with their cash here.

Waterlooplein
MAP Q5

Whether your taste is exotic crafts and jewellery or vintage clothes, you can find them from Monday to Saturday at the city's best flea market – although it's a jumble at the best of times. When you can take no more, escape to the adjacent indoor markets.

 Waterlooplein

Antiekcentrum Amsterdam

Burrow for bargains in this highly browsable and perpetually intriguing indoor warren of antiques and collectibles. When you come up for air, there's also a café where you can rest your weary feet (see p104).

Noordermarkt

There has been a market on this site since 1627. Stretching from the Noordermarkt down the length of the Westerstraat, it is popular with locals who come here on Monday mornings to rummage for unbeatable fabric, accessories, second-hand clothes and books (see p96).

TOP 10 SOUVENIRS

Colourful clogs

1 Clogs
The quintessential Dutch footwear; be in fashion, and be heard.

2 Beer
There's more to Dutch beer than Heineken. They make a fabulous variety of beers in the Netherlands, and you will find many of them at De Bierkoning beer shop (see p91).

3 Bulbs
Check your country's import regulations before packing this floral souvenir into your luggage. You may have to post them instead.

4 Dutch Sweets
Handmade Belgium chocolates and Droste pastilles are both delicious, but salty liquorice is an acquired taste.

5 Cheese
If you don't have time to make it to an out-of-town cheese market, visit De Kaaskamer (see p108) for a mouth-watering selection that's guaranteed to impress more than Edam or Gouda.

6 Condoms
Novelty condoms galore; the city's infamous Condomerie (Warmoesstraat 141) will oblige.

7 Delftware
If you don't manage to snag one of the dishy Dutch, at least you can take home a Dutch dish.

8 Diamonds
Definitely a girl's best friend, but possibly the worst nightmare of whoever has to fork out for them.

9 Jenever
"The father of gin" – the real thing, in a variety of flavours and bottle types.

10 T-shirts/Postcards
You will find no shortage of T-shirts and postcards portraying anything from the utterly sublime to the ridiculous.

🔟 Amsterdam for Free

Schuttersgalerij

1 Schuttersgalerij (Civic Guards Gallery)

Map M4 ▪ **Gedempte Begijnensloot** ▪ **Open 10am–5pm daily**

This large, glass-covered passageway is used to display Amsterdam portraits through the centuries, anything from the stars of Ajax football team to the Civic Guard of Amsterdam's Golden Age. The gallery is attached to – but separate from – the Amsterdam Museum (see pp30–33).

2 Begijnhof

Founded in the 14th century, Amsterdam's delightful Begijnhof (see pp26–7) comprises a huddle of immaculately maintained old houses looking onto a central green. A peaceful and secluded spot, the complex was built as a home for the *begijns* (Beguines) – members of a Catholic sisterhood living as nuns but with the right to return to the secular world.

3 Vondelpark

A welcome splash of greenery, the Vondelpark (see p121) is a favourite with the locals, who come here to ramble and amble, jog and chat, tend their babies and catch free summertime concerts. The park also boasts a wide variety of plants and trees, a network of waterways, a pond, and the wonderful Het Blauwe Theehuis (see p125).

4 Museumplein

Flat as a pancake, the green lawns and gravelled spaces of Museumplein (see p122), stretching out behind the Rijksmuseum (see pp16–19), are used for a variety of outdoor activities, from touring circuses to political protests. Come to see what's happening and ponder the modern memorial to those who perished in Ravensbrück concentration camp (see p50).

5 Concerts

Amsterdam is one of the most popular tourist destinations in Europe and to help entertain its many visitors, the city puts on a wide range of free concerts both outside and inside. Two prime locations are the Concertgebouw (see p122) and the Vondelpark (see p121). For what's happening and where, check out www.iamsterdam.com.

Concertgebouw

6 Ferry across the IJ Harbour

MAP E2 ▪ **De Ruijterkade, behind Centraal Station** ▪ **0900 80 11** ▪ **Ferries to and from Buiksloterweg every 15 min; journey time 5 min** ▪ **www.gvb.nl**

Long Amsterdam's nautical lifeline, the murky waters of the River IJ still hum with river traffic from boats and barges to yachts and freighters. Three free passenger ferries shuttle across the river from behind Centraal Station; the most interesting stop is Buiksloterweg near the EYE (see p131).

7 Rijksmuseum Gardens
Map D5

Adorning several acres, the gardens make for a stunning outdoor gallery. They combine lawns, ponds and sculptures from the original 1901 design with city relics, a giant chess set and a contemporary water maze. This secluded oasis is free to wander and is the perfect setting for ever-changing exhibitions of works by world-famous sculptors (see p17).

8 EYE Film Institute
Sleek and slick and home to some of the city's best art-house cinema, the EYE Film Institute is Amsterdam's proudest modern building. Cinema tickets don't come for free, but exploring this wonderful building doesn't cost anything and neither does the display on the EYE's extensive film collection. Best of all, the views back over the city are simply splendid (see p131).

9 Bloemenmarkt
Amsterdam's world-famous flower market occupies a series of floating barges that march up along the Singel canal. This is the place to come for your bulbs and your blooms, though of course it's the tulips that are the real favourite. The usual suspects can be found on sale here too – all the typical tourist souvenirs, from Dutch clogs to garden gnomes (see pp112–13).

10 Walking Tours
If you are short on time, one of the best introductions to Amsterdam is a guided walking tour. A number of companies offer tours that take in the famous sights and also the hidden gems, with knowledgeable guides who work just for tips. Try the Free Original Alternative tour to take in sights such as street art and the Red Light District, or Original Amsterdam Tours for more sedate attractions (www. originalamsterdamtours.com).

TOP 10 BUDGET TIPS

1 Accommodation
Hotel rooms in Amsterdam can be pricey and limited; be sure to book well ahead to get the best prices (see p143).

2 Eating
One of the many Italian, Indonesian and Chinese restaurants is often the best bet for a budget meal.

3 Drinking
Avoid the bars near Centraal Station and on the Damrak – these are locally known to be high-priced tourist traps.

4 Sights
The I amsterdam City Card (see p142), available for 24-, 48- or 72-hour periods, gives great value on city transport and attractions.

5 Museums
Keen on museums? Save money with the excellent Museumkaart (see p142).

6 Internet
Free internet access and Wi-Fi is commonplace throughout the city and can be found in hotels, cafés, restaurants and bars.

7 Show Tickets
The Stadsschouwburg ticket office on the Leidseplein has great last-minute deals on theatre and show tickets.

8 Shopping
Bargain-hunt at the outdoor markets of Albert Cuypmarkt, Waterlooplein and Noordermarkt (see pp72–3).

9 Transport
Single tickets on public transport are the most expensive option – day passes or the I amsterdam City Card (see p142) are better value for money.

10 Street Entertainment
The best buskers and free concert performances are on Leidseplein.

Street entertainers

TOP 10 Festivals and Events

Rijksmuseum during Nationaal Museumweekend

1 Nationaal Museumweekend
Early Apr

Most of Amsterdam's state-run museums participate in this scheme, run by SMK (Stichting Museumkaart), to offer free or reduced-price entry for one weekend. Details are published through the Tourist Board in March.

2 Bevrijdingsdag
5 May

The day after Herdenkingsdag (Remembrance Day), Liberation Day celebrates the end of the Nazi occupation with speeches, free concerts, markets and festivities throughout the city, in the main squares and parks.

3 Holland Festival
Jun ▪ 020 788 2100
▪ www.hollandfestival.nl

An exciting programme of theatre, music, opera, musical theatre and art at various venues in the city, the Holland Festival has earned itself a prestigious reputation, attracting top-flight performers from the Netherlands and abroad.

4 Grachtenfestival
Aug ▪ 020 421 4542
▪ www.grachtenfestival.nl

National and international stars perform classical music concerts at several locations around the Grachtengordel (see p15) during this 10-day festival. The highlight is a free piano recital given on a barge on Prinsengracht opposite the Pulitzer Hotel. Concerts are also held at Muziekgebouw aan't IJ (see p63).

5 Open Monumentendagen
2nd weekend in Sep ▪ 020 422 2118
▪ www.openmonumentendag.nl

An exciting opportunity to see what lies behind the gabled façades and medieval doorways of some of the city's most historic buildings, which are open to the public for free over this weekend.

6 Open Tuinendagen
3rd weekend in Jun
▪ www.opentuinendagen.nl

During Open Garden Days, some 30 canal-house gardens are open to the public. Visit the green spaces of several museums, like Van Loon (see pp36–7), and take the rare opportunity to see many private gardens. A day ticket includes transport by canal boat to all houses.

7 Jordaan Festival
Sep

This picturesque district makes an ideal setting for an early-autumn festival. The local talent comes out of the woodwork for contests on the corner of Elandsgracht and Marnixstraat, with concerts, parties and fairs – like the one devoted to food in Noordermarkt *(see p96)*.

⑧ Sinterklaas' Parade
2nd or 3rd Sat in Nov
The Christmas festivities start early here. St Nicholas, the Dutch Santa Claus, arrives near St Nicholaaskerk by boat from Spain with his mischievous helpers. Together they throw sweets and *pepernoten* (cinnamon-flavoured biscuits) to the crowds.

⑨ Vondelpark Openluchttheater
Jun–Aug ■ www.openluchttheater.nl
Each summer, Vondelpark's open-air theatre, located in the heart of the park, plays host to a series of free concerts and performances, including dance, music (of all genres), children's theatre and comedy *(see p125)*.

Koningsdag celebrations

⑩ Koningsdag
27 Apr (if Sun, 26 Apr)
On King's Day – Willem-Alexander's birthday – the whole city becomes a gigantic street party. The locals sell bric-a-brac on the streets, public stages are set up all around the city, and people dressed in orange throng the streets. Music blares all day and the party goes on till dawn.

TOP 10 SPECTATOR SPORTS

Dam tot Damloop run

1 Show-Jumping
Amsterdam RAI, Europaplein
Jumping Amsterdam is a series of international indoor competitions (Jan–Feb).

2 Football
Amsterdam ArenA, Bijlmer
See Ajax at their remarkable 50,000-seater stadium (Feb–May, Aug–Dec).

3 Rowing
Numerous competitions including the Head of the Amstel River race (late Mar).

4 Rugby
Bok de Korverweg 6
AAC Rugby Club caters for all ages (Apr–Jun).

5 Cycling
Dam tot Dam Fiets Classic
Road circuit begins and ends at Dam Square (Sep).

6 Hockey
Nieuwe Kalfjeslaan 19, Amstelveen
Amsterdamsche Hockey & Bandy Club are the ones to watch (Sep–May).

7 Korfbal
Sportpark Joos Banckersweg
A cross between netball and basketball. Blauw Wit is the club to watch (Sep–Jun).

8 Running
Olympisch Stadion Stadionplein
Popular runs are the Dam tot Damloop and Amsterdam Marathon (Sep–Oct).

9 Ice Hockey
Sporthal Jaap Edenhal, Radioweg 64
The city supports the popular Amstel Tigers (Oct–late Mar).

10 Skating
Amsterdam Friday Night Skate (if roads are dry), Vondelpark *(see p121)* at 8:30pm, for skilled skaters only (year-round).

Amsterdam Area by Area

Prinsengracht in spring

🔟 Oude Zijde

The streets of the Oude Zijde (Old Side) are packed with historic and beautiful buildings. As the name suggests, this is where Amsterdam has its roots; the city grew from a ribbon of land on the eastern bank of the Amstel between Damrak and Oudezijds Voorburgwal ("before the city wall"). Today, the Oude Zijde incorporates the medieval city, built around the Oude Kerk, and the area to the east. An area of richness and contrasts, within its boundaries lie the Nieuwmarkt (dominated by the Waag, a 15th-century city gate turned weigh-house), the university quarter, Chinatown, the Red Light district, and the superb Joods Historisch Museum.

The Oude Kerk, Oude Zijde

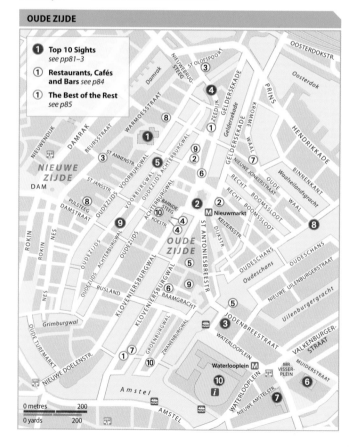

OUDE ZIJDE

1 **Top 10 Sights**
see pp81–3

1 **Restaurants, Cafés and Bars** see p84

1 **The Best of the Rest**
see p85

1 Oude Kerk

The oldest church in Amsterdam has been altered and extended a number of times over the years, producing a heavenly jumble of architectural styles from medieval to Renaissance *(see pp34–5)*.

2 Nieuwmarkt
MAP P3

This vast open square has been a marketplace since the 15th century, and is still the scene of a weekly organic market each Saturday. Alone in the middle stands the bulky Waag (1488), bristling with turrets. The eastern gate in the city's defences, it was originally called St Antoniespoort. In the 17th century, it became a weigh-house and home to numerous guilds (represented on the doors), including the surgeons' guild. It was here that Rembrandt painted his famous *Anatomy Lesson of Dr Nicolaes Tulp* (1632). There were few problems acquiring bodies for dissection, since public executions took place in the Nieuwmarkt.

Nieuwmarkt's centrepiece, the Waag

3 Museum Het Rembrandthuis
MAP Q5 ■ Jodenbreestraat 4 ■ 020 520 0400 ■ Open 10am–5pm daily ■ Closed 27 Apr, 25 Dec ■ Adm ■ www.rembrandthuis.nl

Using the detailed inventory drawn up at Rembrandt's bankruptcy in 1658, the museum has been reconstructed to look just as it did in the artist's time. Of special interest are pictures by his master, Pieter Lastman. One room contains exotic collectibles of the day – spears, shells, Roman busts – as well as Rembrandt's precious art books and a record of his effects *(see p19)*. Daily etching and paint-making demonstrations – at no extra cost – enhance the experience.

Museum Het Rembrandthuis

4 Zeedijk
MAP Q2

Built in the early 1300s, the Zeedijk (sea dyke) was part of Amsterdam's original fortifications. As the city grew, the canals were filled in and the dykes became obsolete. At No. 1 is one of the city's two remaining wooden-fronted houses, dating from the 16th century. Opposite is St Olofskapel, built in 1445 and named for the first Christian king of Norway and Denmark.

5 Red Light District
MAP P2, P3

The world's oldest profession occupies Amsterdam's oldest quarter, De Wallen, bordered by Zeedijk, Kloveniersburgwal, Damstraat and Warmoesstraat. Today, it is one of the city's greatest tourist attractions and a campaign to make the area more attractive was launched in 2007. The council has confined window-prostitutes to two main areas, and encouraged small creative businesses to open up shop in their place.

MODERN-DAY TOLERANCE

In line with the city's tradition of tolerance, the authorities overlook the personal possession and consumption of small quantities of cannabis or marijuana, although they are illegal. Their sale and use at regulated coffeeshops *(see p67)* is officially accepted, but hard drugs and advertising are not. Visit the Hash Marihuana & Hemp Museum **(below)** for a history of hemp.

6 Portuguese Synagogue

MAP R5 ▪ Mr Visserplein 3 ▪ 020 531 0310 ▪ Open Mar, Apr, Sep & Oct: 10am–5pm Sun–Thu, 10am–4pm Fri; May–Aug: 10am–5pm Sun–Fri; Nov & Feb: 10am–5pm Sun–Thu, 10am–2pm Fri; Dec & Jan: 10am–4pm Sun–Thu, 10am–2pm Fri ▪ Closed Sat and Jewish hols ▪ Adm ▪ www.jck.nl/en

The Sephardic Jews, who settled in Amsterdam from the late 16th century, celebrated their new lives in a tolerant society a century later by commissioning Elias Bouman to build this imposing synagogue. It follows a traditional design with the Hechal (Holy Ark), facing Jerusalem, opposite the bema, from where the cantor leads the service. A splendid collection of brocades, ceremonial silverware and manuscripts is on display in the treasury. Tickets to the Jewish Historical Quarter, valid for a month, provide entrance to this synagogue, the Joods Historisch Museum and the Hollandsche Schouwburg *(see p129)*.

7 Joods Historisch Museum

MAP Q5 ▪ Nieuwe Amstelstraat 1 ▪ 020 531 0310 ▪ Open 11am–5pm daily ▪ Closed Yom Kippur, Rosh Hashanah ▪ Adm ▪ www.jck.nl/en

Abel Cahen's prize-winning design for the Jewish Historical Museum (1987) is a perfect blend of old and new: the four synagogues that house it, built by Ashkenazi Jews during the 17th and 18th centuries, are linked by glass-covered walkways. This multi-media museum explains the history and culture of the Jewish community in Holland *(see p50)*. Youngsters will enjoy the Children's Museum.

8 Montelbaanstoren

MAP R3 ▪ Oudeschans 2

The Montelbaanstoren fortified tower was built in 1512 just outside the city wall. Its original purpose was to defend the Dutch fleet; now it houses the city's water authority. The open-work steeple was added by Hendrick de Keyser in 1606, when the city fathers felt that they could at last

Extinguishing candles at the Portuguese Synagogue

Montelbaanstoren

afford the icing on the proverbial cake. It overlooks the Oudeschans (see p56), a lovely canal also from the early 16th century.

⑨ Hash Marihuana & Hemp Museum

MAP P3 ▪ Oudezijds Achterburgwal 148 ▪ 020 624 8926 ▪ Open 10am–10pm daily ▪ Closed 27 Apr ▪ Adm ▪ www.hashmuseum.com

Exhibits in this museum chart the history of *hennep* (hemp) from about 8,000 years ago to the 20th-century drug wars. As *hennep*, it was used for making lace, fishing nets and fabric for sails, and processed by special windmills called *hennepkloppers*. There are displays about smuggling, an array of hookahs and reefers, and a "grow room" where plants are cultivated.

⑩ Nationale Opera & Ballet

MAP Q5 ▪ Waterlooplein 22 ▪ 020 625 5455 ▪ Open noon–6pm Mon–Fri, noon–3pm Sat, Sun & public hols ▪ www.operaballet.nl

The Nationale Opera & Ballet, also called "Stopera", combines the *stadhuis* (town hall) with the city opera and ballet companies' headquarters. This red-brick, marble and glass building was built in 1987 amid controversy, since scores of medieval houses had to be destroyed. In the passage between the two buildings, a bronze button indicates the NAP (Normaal Amsterdams Peil) high water level.

A DAY IN OUDE ZIJDE

▶ MORNING

Start your day with a tour of the **Museum Ons' Lieve Heer op Solder** (see pp24–5), which opens at 10am. Although in the Nieuwe Zijde, it is only a few steps from the **Oude Kerk** (see pp34–5), which you can visit afterwards. Then walk to **Nieuwmarkt** (see p81) for a break at In de Waag (Nieuwmarkt 4), where you can sit, overlooking the square. Afterwards, make your way to Oudezijds Achterburgwal for the **Hash Marihuana & Hemp Museum**. Then follow the main drag of the **Red Light District** (see p81), Oudezijds Voorburgwal, as far as **Bridges Restaurant** (see p64) for lunch.

AFTERNOON

Walk down to peaceful Grimburgwal and the House on the Three Canals. Head east to Oudezijds Achterburgwal and cut through Oudemanhuispoort (stone spectacles mark the entrance), browsing through the second-hand bookstalls as you go. Continue to Jodenbreestraat and the **Museum Het Rembrandthuis** (see p81). After your tour (Monday, Wednesday, Friday or Saturday) pop into **Pintohuis** (see p46) for a glimpse of the painted ceiling. Stop to revive yourself at charming **Café de Sluyswacht** (see p84). From here, there is a lovely canal-side walk, past the **Montelbaanstoren**. Turn left and stroll along **Binnenkant** (see p59) before heading back to your hotel.

Restaurants, Cafés and Bars

1 Bird
MAP P2 ■ Zeedijk 72–74
■ 020 620 1442 ■ €
Those in the know flock here for the tastiest Thai in town. Eat in the restaurant or head out to their snackbar opposite for an utterly authentic experience.

2 Café Cuba
MAP P3 ■ Nieuwmarkt 3
■ 020 627 4919 ■ €
An intriguing ode to the communist country, this long and narrow, darkly lit bar serves fantastic cocktails and pitchers of sangria. There is a pool table at the back.

3 In 't Aepjen
MAP P2 ■ Zeedijk 1 ■ €
This unusual bar is located in one of the oldest wooden houses in the city, built in 1551. Sailors would pay for their stay in monkeys – hence the primate theme.

In 't Aepjen

4 De Bekeerde Suster
MAP P4 ■ Kloveniersburgwal 6-8 ■ 020 423 0112 ■ €
In 1544, the nuns at this cloister started making beer, a tradition revitalized a few years ago – and there's a fine restaurant.

5 Café de Sluyswacht
MAP Q4 ■ Jodenbreestraat 1
■ 020 625 7611 ■ €
Rembrandt sketched this leaning, ex-lock-keeper's house. It has a lovely canal-side terrace at the back.

6 De Engelbewaarder
MAP P4 ■ Kloveniersburgwal 59 ■ 020 625 3772 ■ €
Frequented by hi-brow locals, this convivial bar serves cheap and cheerful food and specialist beers on a peaceful canal-side terrace. Live jazz on Sundays.

7 Captein & Co
MAP Q3 ■ Binnen Bantammerstraat 27 ■ 020 627 8804 ■ €
End a day of sightseeing with a visit to this restaurant overlooking the tranquil Kromme Waal canal.

8 Wijnand Fockink
MAP N3 ■ Pijlsteeg 31
■ 020 639 2695 ■ €
Barely looking a day older than its 1679 origins, this is the best *proeflokaal* (tasting house) in town. The hidden garden is only for use by guests of the Krasnapolski Hotel.

9 Lime
MAP P3 ■ Zeedijk 104
■ 020 639 3020 ■ €
One of the hippest and friendliest bars in the area.

10 Blauw aan de Wal
MAP P4 ■ Oudezijds Achterburgwal 99 ■ 020 330 2257 ■ €€€
An absolute treasure in the heart of the Red Light District, this uropean restaurant should be savoured.

The Best of the Rest

1 Staalstraat
MAP P5

Narrow and extraordinarily pretty Staalstraat boasts two lovely little swing bridges, a platoon of cafés and shops, and delightful canal views.

Fo Guang Shan Temple

2 Fo Guang Shan Temple
MAP P3 ▪ Zeedijk 106–118 ▪ 020 420 2357

This nun-run Chinese Buddhist temple takes pride of place on Zeedijk. Take a peek one afternoon (you can keep your shoes on), or join a tour, held on Saturday afternoons.

3 W139
MAP N3 ▪ Warmoesstraat 139 ▪ 020 622 9434 ▪ Open noon–6pm Mon–Sun ▪ www.w139.nl

Founded in 1979, W139 has evolved from its artist-run squat, anti-establishment roots to become a professional platform for contemporary art.

4 Jacob Hooy & Co
MAP P3 ▪ Kloveniersburgwal 10–12

Established in 1743, this is the best place in town to pick up herbs, homeopathic remedies, teas and essential oils.

5 Joe's Vliegerwinkel
MAP P4 ▪ Nieuwe Hoogstraat 19 ▪ 020 625 0139

Colourful kites, knick-knacks and kitsch trinkets for that perfect present.

6 Latei
MAP P3 ▪ Zeedijk 143

A delightful café cum bric-a-brac store. Ideal for a sandwich, fresh juice, or a decent-sized coffee.

7 Droog Design
MAP P5 ▪ Staalstraat 7A/B ▪ 020 523 5059 ▪ www.droog.com

A group of young Dutch designers have joined forces to form Droog Design. Check it out for witty home accessories and furniture.

8 Tibet
MAP P2 ▪ Lange Niezel 24 ▪ 020 624 1137 ▪ €€

Quite a find in the seedy surrounds of the Red Light District, this restaurant serves food until midnight.

9 Zuiderkerk
MAP P4 ▪ Zuiderkerkhof 72 ▪ 020 689 2565 ▪ Tower: Open Apr–Oct: noon–6pm Mon–Sat ▪ Church closed to the public ▪ Adm ▪ www.westertorenamsterdam.nl

Built 1603–1611 by Hendrick de Keyser, and painted by Monet in 1874. Climb to the top for great city views.

10 Shop de Ville
MAP P5 ▪ Staalstraat 11 ▪ www.shopdeville.nl

This quirky store offers a unique collection of gadgets, toys and jazzy homeware.

Shop de Ville

See map on p80

📥 Nieuwe Zijde

Despite its name, the Nieuwe Zijde (New Side), together with the Oude Zijde, was at the centre of Amsterdam's early maritime settlement. From the boundary between the two, the Nieuwe Zijde extends west to the Singel, and over time it has developed a different character from its neighbour. The medieval city, with its wooden housing, was highly susceptible to fire, and much of the area was burnt down in 1452. During the 19th century, most of its canals were filled in, resulting in lively shopping streets Damrak, Rokin and Nieuwendijk, as well as Kalverstraat, scene of a medieval market. Pockets of history survive – in the network of narrow 14th-century streets off Kalverstraat, the Begijnhof, the 17th-century orphanage that houses the Amsterdam Museum, and, at the heart of the district, Dam Square.

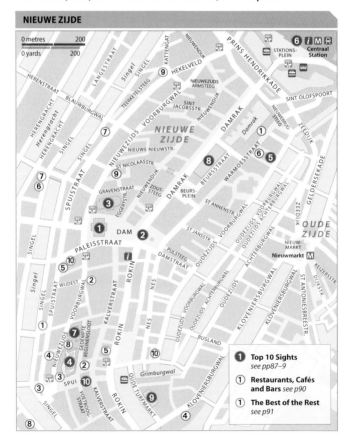

NIEUWE ZIJDE

● Top 10 Sights
see pp87–9

① Restaurants, Cafés and Bars see p90

① The Best of the Rest
see p91

The central hall, or *burgerzaal*, at the Koninklijk Paleis

1 Koninklijk Paleis

Supported by a staggering 13,659 wooden piles, Jacob van Campen's Classical building occupies one side of Dam Square. Designed as the *stadhuis* (town hall), it was transformed into a Royal Palace in 1808 by King Louis Bonaparte. Although it is still used for official functions, such as the wedding reception of Crown Prince Willem-Alexander in February 2002, the present royal family live elsewhere. It is now open to the public *(see pp40–41)*.

Gilded cherub, Nieuwe Kerk

2 Dam Square

Amsterdam's main square is named after the dam on the River Amstel around which the city grew. By the 17th century, it had become the focus of the Dutch trading empire *(see pp40–41)*.

3 Nieuwe Kerk

Wealthy merchant banker Willem Eggert donated his orchard as a site for this Gothic church, as well as a large sum of money for its construction. It was consecrated to Our Lady and St Catherine, but has only ever been called the Nieuwe Kerk – to distinguish it from the Oude Kerk. It has been the setting for the coronation of every Dutch monarch since the early 19th century *(see p41)*.

4 Begijnhof

A charming and secluded courtyard of houses surrounding a tranquil garden in the centre of the city, the Begijnhof was established in the 14th century as a sanctuary for the Beguines lay Catholic sisterhood *(see pp26–7)*.

Begijnhof

5 Museum Ons' Lieve Heer op Solder

This canal house-turned-museum, with its sober decoration and delightful *schuilkerk* (secret Catholic church) hidden within its upper floors, plunges visitors back into the Golden Age *(see pp24–5)*.

6 Centraal Station
MAP P1

■ Stationsplein ■ 0900 9292

Many visitors' experience of Amsterdam begins at Centraal Station, the transport hub of the city, where some 1,400 trains arrive and leave every day. It was built in the 1880s in Neo-Renaissance style by P J H Cuypers and A L van Gendt. Before work on the building could start, three artificial islands had to be constructed with 8,600 wooden piles sunk to support them. The

building blocked Amsterdammers' view of the sea, causing much controversy at the time. The ornate red-brick façade depicts themes of travel, trade and city history, picked out in gold and other colours. Visit the station restaurant, 1e Klas *(see p67)*, to see its fine Art Nouveau setting. A major renovation finished in summer 2018 to coincide with the opening of the Noord/Zuid Metro line.

7 Amsterdam Museum

An excellent place to start a visit to Amsterdam, this museum chronicles how a tiny fishing village on the Amstel river grew into one of the wealthiest and most beautiful cities in the world *(see pp30–33)*.

Monstrance, Museum Ons' Lieve Heer op Solder

8 Beurs van Berlage
MAP N2 ■ Damrak 243
■ 020 530 4141 (exhibitions)
■ Open only during exhibitions
■ Adm ■ www.beursvanberlage.nl

The innovative Stock Exchange building was derided when it was unveiled in 1903, but is now considered a key work of the period. Designed by the pioneer of Dutch modern architecture, H P Berlage, its functional lines are softened by ornamental ironwork and tiled mosaics. The Stock Exchange has moved next door and the building is now used to hold conferences, exhibitions and occasionally concerts. There is a guided tour of the building every second or third Saturday of the month.

Amsterdam's Centraal Station

**Greek terracotta mask,
Allard Pierson Museum**

⑨ Allard Pierson Museum
MAP N5 ■ Oude Turfmarkt 127
■ 020 525 2556 ■ Open 10am–5pm
Tue–Fri, 1–5pm Sat, Sun & public hols
■ Closed 1 Jan, 27 Apr, 25 Dec ■ Adm
■ www.allardpiersonmuseum.nl

Located in a stately Neo-Classical building built in the 1860s as a bank, this small museum was named after the University of Amsterdam's first Professor of Classical Archaeology, and contains its archaeological collection. Fascinating exhibits include Egyptian mummies and sarcophagi, Coptic clothes, Cypriot jewellery, Greek geometric and red-figured pottery, Etruscan metalwork and Roman glassware and statuary.

⑩ Spui
MAP M5

This small square, lined with cafés, bars and bookshops, bursts into life at lunchtime and again in the evening, when people spill out onto the pavement from bars. Cheek by jowl with university buildings, Spui has long been a place where intellectuals gather to drink and debate. There is also a Friday book market. In the Provo riots of the 1960s (see p45), the square was the scene of political protests, during which Carol Kneulman's statue of an urchin, *Het Lieverdje* (Little Darling), was frequently daubed with slogans. At No. 18, Café Hoppe (see p90) is a landmark brown café that has been in business since 1670.

Het Lieverdje, Spui

A DAY IN NIEUWE ZIJDE

▶ MORNING

Spend the morning in the **Amsterdam Museum** (see pp30–33), although a morning is scarcely enough. When you feel like a break, leave the main building and head for the Kalverstraat entrance, where the café-restaurant David and Goliath is on your left. Make sure that you keep your ticket so that you can re-enter the museum without having to pay again. The end of the tour brings you to the excellent museum shop. Rather than leaving by one of the exits, cut through the Civic Guards' Gallery to the **Begijnhof** (see pp26–7), and while away some time in this secluded place. Come out of the Gedempte Begijnensloot entrance and turn the corner into **Spui**, where you might lunch at Café Hoppe (see p90) or Café Luxembourg (Spui 24).

AFTERNOON

After lunch, walk down **Kalverstraat**, the district's main shopping street, to **Dam Square**, where you could visit the **Koninklijk Paleis** (see pp40–41) as well as the **Nieuwe Kerk** (see p41). Then take a break among the tiny shops built into the buttresses of the church in Gravenstraat; at No.18, **De Drie Fleschjes** is one of the oldest *proeflokalen* (tasting houses) for Dutch gin, dating from 1650. When you are revived, walk down **Damrak** past the **Beurs van Berlage** to finish your day at the **Centraal Station**, where you can hop on a tram back to your hotel.

Restaurants, Cafés and Bars

1 De Compagnon
MAP P2 ▪ Guldehandsteeg 17 ▪ 020 620 4225 ▪ €€€

Open for lunch and dinner, De Compagnon serves traditional cuisine using fresh ingredients, with an extensive wine list. It also hosts wine tastings and workshops.

2 Rozenboom
MAP M5 ▪ Rozenboomsteeg 6 ▪ 020 622 5024 ▪ €

This tiny restaurant just off Kalverstraat offers homely Dutch meals, pancakes and the ubiquitous *appeltaart* (apple pie).

3 Café Hoppe
MAP M5 ▪ Spui 18 ▪ 020 420 4420 ▪ €

Open since 1670, this historic brown café, with its lefty past and church pews, was a regular haunt of radical writers and intellectuals in the Provo-fuelled 1960s.

Interior of grand café De Jaren

4 De Jaren
MAP N5 ▪ Nieuwe Doelenstraat 20–22 ▪ 020 625 5771 ▪ €€

Formerly a bank, this modern grand café, with huge windows, serves sandwiches, soups and delicious meals. Sit out on the waterside terrace in summer.

PRICE CATEGORIES

For a three-course meal for one with half a bottle of wine (or equivalent meal), taxes and extra charges.

€ under €30   €€ €30–€45   €€€ over €45

5 Het Schuim
MAP M3 ▪ Spuistraat 189 ▪ 020 638 9357 ▪ €

Art meets alcohol at this large, rustic-style bar, a popular hangout for creative types. Food is served daily until 9:30pm.

6 Getto
MAP P2 ▪ Warmoesstraat 51 ▪ 020 421 5151 ▪ www.getto.nl ▪ €

This bar also has a restaurant which is open in the evenings and serves home-style filling meals. Burgers are a speciality.

7 Greenwoods
MAP M1 ▪ Singel 103 ▪ 020 623 7071 ▪ €

Australian-run, English tearoom-style café that serves great breakfasts and high teas. Service can be slow, but worth the wait.

8 Supperclub
MAP M5 ▪ Singel 460 ▪ 020 344 6400 ▪ www.supperclub.com ▪ €€€

There's a decadent lounge bar in the basement of this hip restaurant-bar. Dress to impress if you want to get inside.

9 Côte Ouest
MAP N4 ▪ Gravenstraat 20 ▪ 020 320 8998 ▪ €€

Set in a pretty alley behind the Nieuwe Kerk, this restaurant specializes in food from Brittany. Try the traditional savoury buckwheat crepes.

10 Kapitein Zeppos
MAP N4 ▪ Gebed Zonder End 5 ▪ 020 624 2057 ▪ €€

Tucked away in a tiny alleyway, this charming restaurant serves French cuisine with Mediterranean touches.

The Best of the Rest

1 Café Gollem
MAP M4 ■ Raamsteeg 4

This beer café serves a wide selection of pilsners, ales and stouts. Chalkboards scribbled with tasty dishes and a comfortable wooden interior, make this a beer lover's paradise.

2 Japanse Winkeltje
MAP M3 ■ Nieuwezijds Voorburgwal 177 ■ 020 627 9523

Japanese crafts centre selling beautiful lacquered and china bowls, sake decanters and kimonos.

Japanse Winkeltje

3 The American Book Center
MAP M5 ■ Spui 12 ■ 020 625 5537

Three floors of magazines, books, newspapers and games. There are also lectures and writers' workshops at the Treehouse annexe, a short walk away.

4 Hay
MAP M4 ■ Spuistraat 281a–c

For stylish retro furniture and home accessories, visit Hay, a shop created by young Danish designers.

5 P G C Hajenius
MAP N3 ■ Rokin 96

Dutchman Hajenius fulfilled his 1826 pipe dream, and his store is now one of Europe's most famous cigar houses. A must for all smoking connoisseurs, but worth a peek just for the Art Deco interior.

6 iinn
MAP M5 ■ Singel 188, 1016 AA ■ 020 627 6337

For an afternoon of pampering, head to this spa where therapists work to Ayurvedic principles. Offers haircare, manicures and pedicures.

7 Puccini Bomboni
MAP M2 ■ Singel 184 ■ 020 427 8341

A chocoholic's paradise! Mouth-watering chocolates often with surprising fillings, such as nutmeg, lemongrass or pepper. You can also feast on big chunks of chocolate.

8 Gastronomie Nostalgie
MAP M4 ■ Nieuwezijds Voorburgwal 361 ■ 020 422 2167

This charming shop sells elegant tableware for special occasions. Stock for sale includes silverware, porcelain and crystal.

9 Bitterzoet
MAP N1 ■ Spuistraat 2 ■ 020 421 2318

This modern club ("Bittersweet" in English) has music nights to suit everybody, from live bands to DJ sets.

10 De Bierkoning
MAP M3 ■ Paleisstraat 125 ■ 020 625 2336

"The Beer King" in the shadow of the Dam's Royal Palace has a fantastic range of beers from all over the world.

De Bierkoning

See map on p86

TOP 10 Western Canal Ring

For many, the Western Canal Ring perfectly encapsulates the city's relaxed yet stylish air. Construction of the Grachtengordel, Amsterdam's ring of four fashionable canals, began here, with the marshy area just beyond reserved by city planner Hendrick Staets for workers and their unpalatable industries; Huguenot refugees who settled here were said to have named it Jardin (Garden), later corrupted to Jordaan, and today it is one of Amsterdam's most fascinating districts. Its narrow streets and oblique canals might seem random, but they followed the course of old paths and drainage ditches. North of the Brouwersgracht lies the revitalized district of Haarlemmerbuurt, and, further afield, the Western Islands, created in the mid-17th century to provide much-needed warehousing.

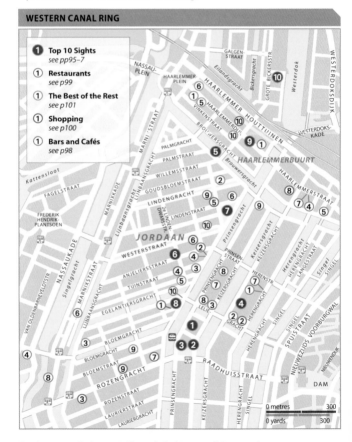

WESTERN CANAL RING

1 **Top 10 Sights**
see pp95–7

1 **Restaurants**
see p99

1 **The Best of the Rest**
see p101

1 **Shopping**
see p100

1 **Bars and Cafés**
see p98

Previous pages Bridge over Leidsegracht looking towards Herengracht

1 Anne Frank House

This thought-provoking museum encompasses the *achterhuis* – the secret hide-out of Anne Frank and her family – as well as background information on the plight of Amsterdam's Jews and racial oppression (*see pp38–9*).

2 Homomonument

MAP L2 ▪ Westermarkt (between Westerkerk and Keizersgracht) ▪ www.homo monument.nl

This first memorial in the world to gay men and women who lost their lives during World War II also pays tribute to homosexuals who are still being oppressed today. The memorial was designed by Dutch artist Karin Daan and was erected in 1987. It consists of three equilateral triangles made of pink granite, one level with the street, one protruding into the Keizersgracht and one slightly raised – symbolising the past, present and future. The pink triangle, originally a badge gay men were forced to wear in Nazi concentration camps, became a symbol of gay pride in the 1970s and '80s.

3 Westerkerk

MAP L2 ▪ 020 624 7766 ▪ Prinsengracht 281 ▪ Church: open 11am–3pm Mon–Fri (Apr–Sep: also Sat); www.westerkerk.nl ▪ Tower: open Apr–Jun: 10am–6pm Mon–Fri (to 8pm Sat); Jul–Aug: 10am–8pm Mon–Sat; Oct: 10am–6pm Mon–Sat; Adm; www. wester torenamsterdam.nl

A demanding climb to the top of the soaring tower of Westerkerk, a landmark close to the heart of every Amsterdammer, rewards you with a thrilling view. Designed by Hendrick de Keyser and completed in 1631, its austere interior is unadorned, except for the ornate organ and its lively painted shutters. A memorial to Rembrandt reminds us that he was buried here, although the

Westerkerk

precise burial site is unknown. Outside the church, notice the poignant, small statue of Anne Frank at the southwest corner.

4 Huis met de Hoofden

MAP L2 ▪ Keizersgracht 123 ▪ Times vary; check website ▪ www.huismetdehoofden.nl

An eye-catching extravaganza, the House with the Heads is named for the six heads on its elaborate step-gabled façade. Each head represents a Classical god – Apollo, Ceres, Mars, Minerva, Diana and Bacchus. Built in 1622, its Dutch Renaissance design is attributed to Hendrick and Peter de Keyser. The house is scheduled to reopen in autumn 2018. It will now be home to the unique Bibliotheca Philosophica Hermetica or the Ritman Library, founded by Joost

Bust of Mercury, Huis met de Hoofden

Ritman. The library will also host debates and concerts.

The junction of Prinsengracht and Brouwersgracht

5 Brouwersgracht
MAP D1

If you stand at the breezy junction of Brouwersgracht and Prinsengracht, you will get terrific views in all directions. Today, Brouwersgracht, with its pretty bridges and picturesque houseboats, is a romantic's (and photographer's) delight, but if a 17th-century *brouwer* (brewery worker) could see it now, he would be astonished to find that the spout-gabled warehouses of this once reeking industrial canal had been converted into the smartest of private housing – particularly fine examples of which you can see at Nos. 188–194.

Jordaanoproer memorial, Noordermarkt

6 Jordaan
MAP K3

Quirky and characterful, with an intimate, easy-going atmosphere all of its own, the Jordaan is a dense patch of small-scale streets and canals peppered with interesting shops and galleries, charming *hofjes* (almshouses) and inviting brown cafés. Bounded by Prinsengracht and Lijnbaansgracht to the east and west, and Brouwersgracht and Looiersgracht to the north and south, it was built for the working classes who served in the Grachtengordel *(see p15)*.

7 Noordermarkt
MAP D2 ■ Noordermarkt flea market: open 9am–1pm Mon ■ Boerenmarkt: open 9am–4pm Sat

By the entrance to the Noorderkerk *(see p54)*, a sculpture by Sofie Hupkens commemorates the Jordaan riot of 1934, in which seven people died protesting cuts in unemployment benefits. Today, the square comes to life during the Monday flea market and the Saturday *boerenmarkt* (farmers' market).

8 The Amsterdam Tulip Museum
MAP L2 ■ Prinsengracht 116 ■ 020 421 0095 ■ Open 10am–6pm daily ■ Closed 27 Apr, 25 Dec ■ Adm ■ www.amsterdamtulipmuseum.nl

Tulips were first introduced to the Netherlands in the late 16th century,

---

ZON'S AND DE STAR HOFJES

Secretive and intimate, Amsterdam's *hofjes* – almshouses for the needy built by wealthy merchants in the 17th and 18th centuries – are part of the city's charm. Unobtrusive street entrances lead to pretty houses, some of which are still used for their original purpose. Two of the most delightful *hofjes* are Zon's and De Star on the Prinsengracht. Both *hofjes* are open to visitors from Monday to Friday.

starting a love affair that is still going strong today. The museum tells the story of the "world's most dangerous flower" through exhibits that document tulip cultivation and interactive displays that trace the history of the modern flower from its wild beginnings. Visitors can have bulbs shipped to the US or EU.

9 Haarlemmerbuurt

MAP D1

The bustling streets of this stalwart residential neighbourhood have seen the arrival of all manner of shops, mixing bric-a-brac with haute couture, New Age with funky furniture and specialist food with local groceries. On Haarlemmerstraat is West-Indisch Huis, once headquarters of the Dutch West India Company (see p47). To the west is Haarlemmerpoort, peaceful Westerpark (see p61) and Westergasfabriek, the former gasworks-turned-arts-centre.

Western Islands

10 Western Islands

MAP D1 ■ www.oawe.nl

The man-made Western Islands have a remote, bracing quality. Comprising Bickerseiland, Prinseneiland and Realeneiland, they were created in the early 17th century to accommodate shipyards and warehouses. Large-scale development has since taken place, and modern housing now co-exists with white wooden draw-bridges. The area's many artists work from warehouse studios, and open their doors to the public in May in odd-numbered years for the Open Ateliers Westelijke Eilanden.

EXPLORING THE WESTERN CANAL RING

▶ MORNING

Beat the queues and be first to arrive at the **Anne Frank House** (see pp38–9), which opens at 9am. Afterwards, you could take a contemplative walk along Prinsengracht to the Western Islands, perhaps first climbing the tower of **Westerkerk** (see p95). On the way, drop in on two peaceful hofjes, **Zon's** (Nos. 159–171) and **De Star** (Nos. 855–899). For refreshment, visit **Papeneiland**, a tiny brown café founded in 1642, at the junction of Prinsengracht and Brouwersgracht.

On the Western Islands, stroll round **Prinseneiland** and along **Zandhoek** on Realeneiland, stopping for lunch at De Gouden Reael (Zandhoek 14). Families will enjoy Dierencapel, the children's farm on **Bickerseiland**.

AFTERNOON

En route to the Jordaan, hardened shoppers must first stop in Haarlemmerbuurt, with its mix of shops, both smart and tatty. Don't miss a peek at over-the-top **Café Dulac** (Haarlemmerstraat 118), and the world's narrowest restaurant, **De Groene Lanteerne** (Haarlemmerstraat 43).

Spend a couple of hours exploring the endlessly picturesque Jordaan, then join today's trendy young Jordaanese in one of the cafés around **Noordermarkt**, such as Finch (see p98) or Proust (No. 4), or the delightfully kitsch Café Nol (Westerstraat 109). If you're looking for somewhere to have dinner, head for Boca's (see p99).

See map on p94

Bars and Cafés

1 't Arendsnest
MAP M1 ▪ Herengracht 90
▪ 020 421 2057 ▪ www.arendsnest.nl

The place to discover Dutch beer, with over 350 varieties from 50 breweries and micro-breweries. Group tastings can be arranged via the website.

2 Duende
MAP C2 ▪ Lindengracht 62
▪ 020 420 6692 ▪ €

Release your inner gypsy in this busy tapas bar in the Jordaan. Authentic atmosphere, value for money, and live Flamenco music. Olé!

3 Café P96
MAP L1 ▪ Prinsengracht 96
▪ 020 622 1864

This peaceful bar opens around 8pm in the evenings and stays open later than most. The premises extend in the summer to an outdoor terrace on a fairy-lit barge.

4 Harlem
MAP D2 ▪ Haarlemmerstraat 77 ▪ 020 330 1498

This rustic café serves wholesome "soul food" plus hearty sandwiches and fruit shakes.

5 't Smalle
MAP L1 ▪ Egelantiersgracht 12
▪ 020 623 9617

Originally a liquor distillery, this brown bar is now a discerning wine-café. A must-visit.

Café Finch

6 Café Finch
MAP D2 ▪ Noordermarkt 5
▪ 020 626 2461

This small watering-hole on the edge of scenic Noordermarkt can get decidedly crowded. On warmer summer days, the hip local clientele spills out onto the square.

7 Stout!
MAP D2 ▪ Haarlemmerstraat 77 ▪ 020 616 3664 ▪ €€€

Minimalist café drawing a hip crowd who come for the latest trends in international cuisine and the fine wines. Book ahead.

8 Café Sound Garden
MAP J3 ▪ Marnixstraat 164–166 ▪ 020 620 2853

Don't let the tattoos, piercings and grunge factor put you off. This bar has a great atmosphere, a large waterside terrace and some unusual beers on tap, too.

9 Tabac
MAP D2 ▪ Brouwersgracht 101
▪ 020 622 4413

Tabac used to be a brown café but has succumbed to the lounge trend.

10 Café de Twee Zwaantjes
MAP L2 ▪ Prinsengracht 114
▪ 020 625 2729

Open from mid-afternoon until the early hours, "The Two Swans" is an authentic Jordaan bar. Enjoy a drink while you listen to accordion music.

Canal-side seating at 't Smalle

Restaurants

PRICE CATEGORIES

For a three-course meal for one with half
a bottle of wine (or equivalent meal),
taxes and extra charges.

€ under €30 €€ €30–€45 €€€ over €45

---

1 Balraj
MAP D1 ■ Haarlemmerdijk 28
■ 020 625 1428 ■ €

The sister of Beatrix, former Queen
of the Netherlands, is a regular
diner at this well-priced restaurant
that has been offering some of the
best Indian food in town since 1977.

2 De Bolhoed
MAP L1 ■ Prinsengracht 60
■ 020 626 1803 ■ €€

Undoubtedly one of the most
charming restaurants in the area.
Delicious, well-priced vegetarian
(and vegan) food with a wicked
dessert selection, served in a
quirky canal-side location.

3 Restaurant Black and Blue
MAP L2 ■ Leliegracht 46
■ 020 625 0807 ■ €€

This is a fantastic steakhouse
thanks to its dynamic combination
of organic meats and charcoal grill.

4 Foodism
MAP B3 ■ Nassaukade 122 ■ 020
486 8137 ■ www.foodism.nl ■ €€

Excellent Mediterranean cuisine for
a decent price can be found here.
The calamari and grilled marinated
lamb are highly recommended.
Friendly service.

5 Belhamel
MAP D2 ■ Brouwersgracht 60
■ 020 622 1095 ■ €€€

Enjoy one of the most stunning canal
views in the city in an equally superb
Art Noveau dining room. However,
the real show-stealer is the food –
the excellent French cuisine, with
Dutch and other European influences,
lives up to its elegant surroundings.

6 Semhar
MAP J2 ■ Marnixstraat 259–
261 ■ 020 638 1634 ■ €

A friendly spot serving Ethopian and
Eritrean food. Meals are served with
enjera (Ethiopian pancakes). Try the
exotic beers or Ethiopian coffee.

7 Spingaren
MAP M1 ■ Herengracht 88 ■ 020
624 9635 ■ www.spingaren.nl ■ €€

Enjoy a plateful of delicious homemade
charcuterie, paired with a glass of
wine or beer at this restaurant.

Spingaren Restaurant

8 Spanjer & Van Twist
MAP L2 ■ Leliegracht 60
■ 020 639 0109 ■ €

The perfect place to rest those
weary feet. Hole yourself up for
the afternoon in the second-floor
window seat.

9 Toscanini
MAP C2 ■ Lindengracht 75
■ 020 623 2813 ■ €€€

Despite its quiet location and
deceptive size (it's huge inside), this
superb Italian restaurant gets quickly
booked up. The delicious dishes are
cooked in an open kitchen.

10 Boca's
MAP D2 ■ Westerstraat 30
■ 020 820 3727 ■ €€

Hip and trendy Boca's specializes in
mouthwatering sharing platters, as
snacks, for lunch or a light dinner.

See map on p94

Shopping

1 Quinta
MAP K2 ▪ Nieuwe Leliestraat 4

This quirky little wine store is the city's only one selling authentic absinthe. Alternatively, try the traditional Dutch *jenever* (gin) as well as wines on tap. Bring your own bottle to fill or buy one at the store.

2 Big Shoe
MAP L2 ▪ Leliegracht 12

Fashionable footwear for people with big feet!

3 SPRMRKT
MAP J3
▪ Rozengracht
191–193

Spacious and perpetually intriguing, this store is an absolute must for style aficionados who have a discerning eye for retro clothing and accessories, furniture and fabrics.

4 Back Beat
MAP L1 ▪ Egelantiersstraat 19

Jools Holland and Mick Jagger are two famous names to have popped into this new and second-hand record/CD shop specializing in jazz, soul, funk and R&B. Rare collector's items are to be had, too.

Back Beat

5 D.E. Jongejans
MAP D2 ▪ Noorderkerkstraat 18

Vintage frames specialist selling a fascinating selection of eyewear dating from the 1800s onwards. If it's shut, just check out the window display.

6 Mechanisch Speelgoed
MAP D2 ▪ Westerstraat 67
▪ Closed Wed

A fascinating, nostalgia-inducing collection of mechanical toys and good old-fashioned children's playthings. Simply put: life before Xbox.

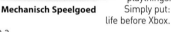

Mechanisch Speelgoed

7 Kitsch Kitchen
MAP K3 ▪ Rozengracht 8–12

A rainbow of colourful accessories for cooks and kitchens is on offer here. There is a good selection of fun kid's toys, including Mexican *piñatas*.

8 Casa Bocage
MAP D2
▪ Haarlemmerstraat 111A

A Portuguese delicatessen, Casa Bocage sells authentic cheeses, sausages, olive oils, sardines, tuna and wines, as well as pastries and salads.

9 Pasta Panini
MAP K3 ▪ Rozengracht 82

A fabulous Italian deli. Great for freshly filled ciabattas at lunchtime or hand-made pasta for supper. Plus a tantalizing range of cookies, soup, sauces and wine.

10 papabubble
MAP D1 ▪ Haarlemmerdijk 70

The confectionery artisans in this store produce their unique, hand-crafted sweets on site. Tahitian lime and bergamot are just some of the flavours waiting to be discovered.

The Best of the Rest

Art Deco cinema screen at The Movies

1 The Movies
MAP D1
■ Haarlemmerdijk 161–163

A fixture in Amsterdam, this Art Deco cinema has been around since 1912, complete with a restaurant and café. It shows some mainstream films but specializes in alternative and art-house cinema.

2 Architectura & Natura
MAP L2 ■ Leliegracht 22

Bookshop and publisher specializing in architecture, gardening and natural history. Knowledgeable staff and a wide selection of English-language books.

3 't Geveltje
MAP J2 ■ Bloemgracht 170

Beginners and pros jam together every Thursday night in the Jordaan's famous jazz bar for musicians and jazz aficionados alike.

4 GO Gallery
MAP L1 ■ Prinsengracht 64

Friendly neighbourhood gallery hosting shows with figurative and abstract art by Dutch and international artists.

5 Weldraad
MAP D1 ■ Haarlemmerdijk 147
■ 020 223 2800

If you enjoy knitting, stock up on fine yarns at Weldraad. The shop offers a colourful selection of ecologically produced woollen, cotton and silk yarns.

6 Two for Joy
MAP D1 ■ Haarlemmerdijk 182
■ 020 221 9552

This small, independent roasting company and café serves up some of the best coffee in town. Cakes, breakfast and lunch are available, as are various bags of beans to enjoy.

7 I Love Vintage
MAP K4 ■ Prinsengracht 201
■ Open 9:30am–6pm Mon–Sat, noon–5pm Sun

A boutique like no other in the city, this has designs ranging from 1980s retro to 1920s classics in all sizes.

8 Pancake Bakery
MAP L1 ■ Prinsengracht 191

Although unashamedly touristy, you could do a lot worse than this restaurant in a former 17th-century warehouse named "Hope".

9 Paradox
MAP K2
■ Eerste Bloemdwarsstraat 2

A paradox in itself, this coffeeshop shows few traces of serving "the herb". Fresh fruit and vegetable shakes, healthy food and a bright interior make it a perfect place for breakfast or lunch.

10 Small World
MAP D1 ■ Binnen Oranjestraat 14 ■ 020 420 2774

Simply the best quick-stop for sandwiches, carrot cake and other delicious offerings.

See map on p94

🔟 Central Canal Ring

Felix Meritis, from the canal

Amsterdam's Golden Age canals, Herengracht, Keizersgracht and Prinsengracht, are at their most impressive in this central section of the Grachtengordel, which culminates in the stretch known as the Golden Bend. This is where the wealthiest Amsterdammers built stately houses in the 1660s, often purchasing more than one plot. One of these opulent houses, Het Grachtenhuis, is now a museum, tracing the history of the construction of the canal ring. The intimate cross-streets that run between these three canals, De Negen Straatjes (The Nine Streets), enticingly display the city's talent for creative retail. Cutting through this elegant district is the main thoroughfare, Leidsestraat, which leads to the brash and lively entertainment hub, Leidseplein.

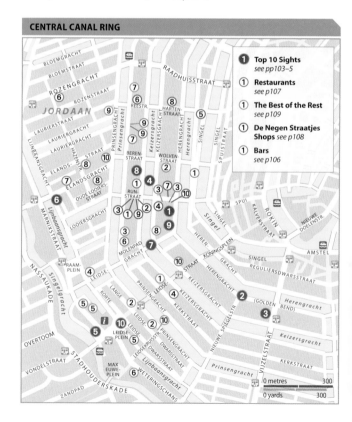

CENTRAL CANAL RING

1 **Top 10 Sights**
see pp103–5

1 **Restaurants**
see p107

1 **The Best of the Rest**
see p109

1 **De Negen Straatjes Shops** see p108

1 **Bars**
see p106

1 Cromhouthuis

MAP L5 ■ Herengracht 368
■ 020 624 2436 ■ Open 11am–5pm
Tue–Sun (from 10am during special
exhibitions) ■ Closed 1 Jan, 27 Apr,
26 Dec ■ Adm ■ www.cromhouthuis.nl

A lovely stretch of Herengracht
is found between Huidenstraat
and Leidsestraat, particularly
Nos. 364–370 – four houses built
by Philips Vingboons in 1662.
Built for the Cromhout family,
No. 368 with its early 18th-century
interior, has been beautifully
restored. The top floor houses a
small Bible museum and a peaceful
garden that has a biblical theme.

2 Golden Bend

MAP M6 ■ Kattenkabinet:
Herengracht 497 ■ 020 626 9040
■ Open 10am–5pm Mon–Fri, noon–
5pm Sat–Sun ■ Closed 1 Jan, 27 Apr,
25 Dec ■ Adm ■ www.kattenkabinet.
nl/en

So named because of the concentration
of wealth amongst its first residents,
this stretch of the Herengracht
between Vijzelstraat and Leidsestraat
feels grand. Quite a few mansions
have intricate façades built of
sandstone instead of brick – the
cheaper alternative. Look out for
Louis XIV-style No. 475, said to be
Amsterdam's most beautiful house;
and No. 476, elegantly restyled in
the 1730s and topped with an
eagle. No. 497 is open to the public,
but you have to like cats: it's the
Kattenkabinet, a unique museum
devoted to cats in art. Be careful not
to trip over one of the many felines.

Kattenkabinet, Golden Bend

Cromhouthuis

3 Stadsarchief Amsterdam

MAP 4 F2 ■ Vijzelstraat 32
■ Tram 16, 24, 25 ■ 020 251 1511
■ Open 10am–5pm Tue–Fri, noon–5pm
Sat–Sun ■ Closed 1 Jan, 27 Apr, 25 Dec
■ www.amsterdam.nl/stadsarchief

The Stadsarchief houses the city's
municipal archives and occupies a
monumental building designed by
the Amsterdamse School architect
De Bazel. It was completed in 1926
and is full of original features.
One of the largest buildings in
the city centre, it was originally the
headquarters of the Netherlands
Trading Corporation (now ABN
Amro). Treasures from the archives
are on display in the former bank
vaults downstairs.

4 De Negen Straatjes

MAP L4

Nestling in the centre of the canal
ring are these three parallel rows
of cross-streets bordered by Singel
and Prinsengracht to east and
west, and Raadhuisstraat and
Leidsegracht to north and south.
Known collectively as The Nine
Streets, these charming roads were
once a centre for the leather trade.
Today, they are packed with amusing
and eccentric shops such as De
Witte Tandenwinkel, which sells all
kinds of toothbrushes *(see p108)*. In
Gasthuismolensteeg, don't miss the
Brilmuseum at No. 7, an enchanting
museum-shop devoted to spectacles
(open noon–5pm Wed–Sat).

Café Americain at the Hampshire Hotel – Amsterdam American

5 Hampshire Hotel – Amsterdam American

MAP C5 ■ Leidsekade 97
■ 020 556 3000

One of Leidseplein's landmarks is this one-off Dutch interpretation of Art Nouveau by Willem Kromhout (1902), which foretold the Amsterdam School of architecture. The hotel's famous Café Americain, with its stained-glass windows and glass parasol lampshades, offers some of the best Art Nouveau design in the city, all for the price of a coffee. The literati crowd may have disappeared, but it's a welcome haven from the hustle and bustle of Leidseplein.

6 Antiekcentrum Amsterdam

MAP J5 ■ Elandsgracht 109
■ Open 11am–6pm Mon, Wed–Fri, 11am–5pm Sat–Sun ■ www. antiekcentrumamsterdam.nl

If the shops of the Spiegelkwartier (see p113) are too expensive and rarified, try searching for antiques in this warren of stalls occupying a vast network of ground-floor rooms in a block of houses near the Looiersgracht (Tanners' Canal). With more than 10,000 objects, this is the largest collection of art and antiques in Holland. The stall-holders host bridge sessions, which are open to all.

7 Leidsegracht

MAP K6

For dream canal houses in pristine condition, look no further than sophisticated Leidsegracht, one of the city's most sought-after addresses. At Herengracht 394, on the corner with Leidsegracht, notice the fine wall plaque depicting characters from a medieval legend – the four Heemskinderen on their horse Beyaart. Another plaque, at No. 39, shows Cornelis Lely, who drew up the original plans for draining the Zuiderzee.

8 Felix Meritis Building

MAP L4 ■ Keizersgracht 324
■ 020 627 9477 ■ www.felix.meritis.nl

The splendid Neo-Classical façade of this building comes as a surprise on gabled Keizersgracht. Designed in 1787 by Jacob Otten Husly as a

---

HOUSEBOATS

Around 2,500 houseboats are called "home" in Amsterdam, but it was only after World War II, when there was a severe housing shortage, that they became popular. They are linked to the city's electricity and water supplies and sewage is pumped into an onshore facility. Visit the Woonbootmuseum (Houseboat Museum) opposite Prinsengracht 296 to find out more.

science and arts centre (the name Felix Meritis means "happiness through merit"), it flourished until the late 19th century. Later, it became headquarters of the Dutch Communist Party (CPN), and in the 1970s was home to the avant-garde Shaffy Theatre Company. The building underwent a major renovation in 2017, but reopened with a programme of events in autumn 2018.

⑨ Het Grachtenhuis
MAP L6 ■ Herengracht 386 ■ 020 421 1656 ■ Open 10am–5pm Tue–Sun ■ Closed 27 Apr ■ Adm ■ www.hetgrachtenhuis.nl

This ornate canal house, designed by Philips Vingboons in 1663–1665, was home to several generations of merchants and bankers. The rooms tell the story of the creation of Amsterdam's canal ring. Its ground floor has been restored to its former 18th-century splendour.

Historical town planning displays, Het Grachtenhuis

⑩ Leidseplein
MAP C5

One of the city's main tourist hubs. Sophisticated it is not, tacky and fun it is, especially in summer, when buskers, street performers, family pop groups and lone fire-eaters keep the throngs amused. A natural gathering place, it is packed with fast-food stalls, cafés and smoking coffeeshops. Nightspots Melkweg, Paradiso and Holland Casino are close at hand, while for a more reflective diversion you can play chess on a giant outdoor chessboard in adjacent Max Euweplein (see p121).

EXPLORING THE CENTRAL CANAL RING

▶ MORNING

This compact area is focused on Amsterdam's most famous canals, so why not start the day with a canal tour. Amsterdam Canal Cruises start and end on Stadhouderskade, opposite the Heineken Brewery. From here, it's a short walk to **Leidseplein** and welcome refreshment at the **Café Americain**.

Leaving the hubbub of Leidseplein, walk along Prinsengracht (passing the Paleis van Justitie, once the city orphanage) to elegant **Leidsegracht**. If there's time, investigate the antiques market, **Antiekcentrum Amsterdam**, on Elandsgracht. For lunch, try brown cafés **Van Puffelen** or **Het Molenpad**, or healthy fare at Goodies (see pp106–7).

AFTERNOON

Plunge into **De Negen Straatjes** (see p103) for some more serious shopping in its frivolous shops. You may not be able to resist the cakes and chocolate on offer at Chocolaterie Pompadour (see p108). Pop into the **Houseboat Museum**, on Prinsengracht opposite Elandsgracht, to marvel at how a bargeman and his family could have lived in such a tiny space. Then cross to Herengracht, which you will have seen earlier from the water, and stroll along, admiring its architectural gems around the **Cromhouthuis** and **Golden Bend** (see p103). Rest your weary feet at **Walem's** canal-side terrace (see p106), while enjoying some nibbles and cocktails.

See map on p102 ←

Bars

1 Proeflokaal A. van Wees
MAP L4 ▪ Herengracht 319
▪ 020 625 4334

One of the smarter *proeflokalen* (tasting houses) in the city – and unlike the rest, Proeflokaal A. van Wees stays open until late. Collapse on the couches after knocking back the liquors and *jenever* (gin).

Proeflokaal A. van Wees

2 Pulitzer's Bar
MAP L3 ▪ Keizersgracht 234
▪ 020 523 5235

This sophisticated, Art Deco-style bar is known for its cosy atmosphere and creative cocktails that are inspired by F Scott Fitzgerald's *The Great Gatsby*. There is also a selection of snacks. Sit by the window for wonderful canal views or relax in one of the armchairs by the fire.

3 Café de Pels
MAP L5 ▪ Huidenstraat 25

A low-key, easy-going neighbourhood bar – locals read the papers at the big table by the window. The café is a great place to recover from a hangover on a Sunday; breakfast is served until 1:30pm.

4 De Zotte
MAP K6 ▪ Raamstraat 29
▪ 020 626 8694

This Belgian bar (named "The Fool") has a huge range of beers. Delicious food helps to soak it all up.

5 Lux
MAP K6 ▪ Marnixstraat 403

Split-level, late-opening designer bar. DJs spin every night.

6 Het Molenpad
MAP K5 ▪ Prinsengracht 653
▪ 020 625 9680

A charming brown bar near the Frozen Fountain *(see p109)* and the Leidsestraat – equally suitable for design lovers and the shopped-out.

7 Vyne
MAP K4 ▪ Prinsengracht 411

Wine bar-cum-Italian delicatessen with trademark interior by architect firm Concrete.

8 Café Saarein
MAP K4 ▪ Elandsstraat 119

Once an infamous women-only bar, now men are welcome. Quiet during the week, rowdy at weekends. There is a pool table and good bar food, too.

9 Van Puffelen
MAP K3 ▪ Prinsengracht 377
▪ 020 624 6270

The rich and beautiful flock to this elegant haunt – the biggest brown bar in town.

10 Walem
MAP L6 ▪ Keizersgracht 449

One of the city's original designer bars, this was the creation of renowned Dutch architect, Gerrit Rietveld. Inside, it's bright and minimalist; outside, there are charming terraces.

Tables by the canal at Walem

Restaurants

PRICE CATEGORIES
For a three-course meal for one with half a bottle of wine (or equivalent meal), taxes and extra charges.

€ under €30   €€ €30–€45   €€€ over €45

1 Restaurant Vinkeles
MAP L4 ■ Keizersgracht 384
■ 020 530 2010 ■ €€€

Housed in the sumptuous Dylan hotel *(see p144)*, this Michelin-starred restaurant is world famous for exciting, modern French cuisine.

2 Bojo
MAP D5 ■ Lange Leidsedwarsstraat 49–51 ■ 020 622 7434 ■ €

Inexpensive, informal and Indonesian, Bojo keeps going after most of the city's other restaurants have gone to bed.

3 Goodies
MAP L5 ■ Huidenstraat 9
■ 020 625 6122 ■ €

A culinary delight in the heart of The Nine Streets. Healthy soups, salads and sandwiches by day; the perfect pasta by night.

4 Los Pilones
MAP L6 ■ Kerkstraat 63
■ 020 320 4651 ■ €€

This Mexican cantina is small, but authentic. Savour the home cooking between slams of tequila.

5 Sumo
MAP K6 ■ Kleine Gartmanplantsoen 17 ■ 020 423 5131 ■ €€

The Japanese interior is matched by an all-you-can-eat menu of sushi, hand rolls and curries. For the location, the price is very reasonable.

6 Pesca Theatre of Fish
MAP J3 ■ Rozengracht 133
■ 020 344 5136 ■ €€

Enjoy the fish of your choice paired with a fine wine or a local beer at this restaurant that offers a novel dining experience. Select the fish you want from the market stall, which will then be prepared while you are seated.

7 Balthazar's Keuken
MAP K4 ■ Elandsgracht 108
■ 020 420 2114 ■ Open Wed–Sat ■ €€€

Book ahead for this unique restaurant, which only serves a set three-course menu.

Balthazar's Keuken

8 Rakang
MAP K4 ■ Elandsgracht 29–31
■ 020 627 5012 ■ €€

Totally authentic Thai; one of the best of its kind in the city. Those in the know head to their cheaper, equally delicious takeaway next door.

9 Envy
MAP K4 ■ Prinsengracht 381
■ 020 344 6407 ■ €€€

This is one of Amsterdam's finest offerings. The chefs expertly combine flavours to create superb Mediterranean delicacies.

10 Fou Fow Ramen
MAP K4 ■ Elandsgracht 2A
■ 020 845 0544 ■ €

A trendy noodle bar serving delicious ramen noodles. Menu includes *tonkotsu* (pork) noodle soup, edamame and *gyoza* (dumplings).

See map on p102 ←

De Negen Straatjes Shops

Huge selection of Dutch cheeses at De Kaaskamer

1 De Kaaskamer
MAP K5 ▪ Runstraat 7

For cheese with a capital C, try "The Cheese Chamber", where there are over 200 different kinds of one of Holland's best exports. If it isn't here, it probably doesn't exist.

2 Burgelijk Amsterdams Burger Bar
MAP L5 ▪ Runstraat 1

Compose your own virtuoso, succulent burger – beef, chicken, or veggie, with a choice of cheese and toppings, accompanied by chunky, homemade chips.

3 Skins Cosmetics
MAP K5 ▪ Runstraat 9
▪ www.skins.nl

An exclusive range of perfumes and cosmetics are on offer in this stark and laboratory-like shop.

4 Van Ravenstein
MAP L5 ▪ Keizersgracht 359

Exclusive boutique selling designer clothing by Dutch, French, English and Belgian designers including Dries van Noten.

5 Brilmuseum/ Brillenwinkel
MAP L3 ▪ Gasthuismolensteeg 7

This fascinating spectacles museum and shop, housed in a 1620 building, explores the history of glasses and sells vintage frames as well as contemporary models.

6 Pontifex
MAP K3 ▪ Reestraat 20

This tiny waxworks gives Madame Tussauds a run for their money, with a colourful range of candles of every type imaginable. Adjoining are the premises of the rather spooky doll doctor, Kramer.

7 Chocolaterie Pompadour
MAP L5 ▪ Huidenstraat 12

You can pile on the calories just staring at the window display of this chic chocolatier. Try the famous homemade chocolates or Pompadour's exquisite tarts.

8 McLennan's Pure Silk
MAP L3 ▪ Hartenstraat 22

From crepe de chine to luscious raw silk, this is the place to come to for a huge range of luxurious items – the owners buy their silks from China, France, Italy, and Thailand.

9 De Witte Tandenwinkel
MAP L5 ▪ Runstraat 5

A veritable ode to the tooth, this shop specializes in every shape or size of toothbrush imaginable, and is sure to take your (bad) breath away. Mouthy Mick Jagger has even dropped by.

10 Zipper
MAP L5 ▪ Huidenstraat 7

Immaculately displayed vintage second-hand accessories and clothes. Also at Nieuwe Hoogstraat 8.

The Best of the Rest

1 Bagels & Beans
MAP L5 ■ Keizersgracht 504

American-style freshly baked cookies and cheesecake, freshly squeezed juices and decent-sized cups of coffee.

2 Ben & Jerry's
MAP K6 ■ Leidsestraat 90

Treat your inner child to some seriously delicious ice cream.

3 Frozen Fountain
MAP K5 ■ Prinsengracht 645

This is arguably Amsterdam's most important designer store and exhibition space for furniture and home accessories. It has an international reputation for its cutting-edge designs and fresh talent.

4 Urban Home & Garden Tours
062 168 1918 ■ www.uhgt.nl/en

Garden designer André Ancion gives 3-hour English-language walking tours delving behind the façades of some of Amsterdam's most impressive canal houses.

5 Melkweg
MAP K6 ■ Lijnbaansgracht 234A
■ 020 531 8181 ■ www.melkweg.nl

Known in the 1970s as an alternative cultural meeting place, today this former milk factory hosts live music events. Plus there's a cinema, theatre, café-bar, gallery, upstairs bar and video room (see p63).

Melkweg cultural centre

6 Paradiso
MAP C5 ■ Weteringschans 6–8
■ 020 626 4521 ■ www.paradiso.nl

One of Amsterdam's best-loved live music spots. Velvet Underground and Macy Gray have played in this former church. The upstairs hall often has unknowns before they go big.

7 Hotel Pulitzer
MAP K3
■ Prinsengracht 315–331

August, at this prestigious hotel, is the time when hampers and champagne come out in full force. A floating stage is set up out front for the unmissable Grachtenfestival's open-air classical concerts (see p76).

Hotel Pulitzer

8 Huis Marseille
MAP L5 ■ Keizersgracht 401
■ 020 531 8989 ■ www.huismarseille.nl

A museum of photography with a programme ranging from historical exhibitions to contemporary work.

9 Raïnaraï
MAP K3 ■ Prinsengracht 252

An utterly charming Algerian deli producing delicious, authentic dishes using spices imported from the North African country. Takeaway, but a few seats inside.

10 Japan Inn
MAP D5 ■ Leidsekruisstraat 4

Small in size but big in popularity, this place serves excellent sushi.

See map on p102

TOP 10 Eastern Canal Ring

The Grachtengordel was extended further east to reach the Amstel in the 1660s, making new plots of land available for wealthy merchants to build their luxurious, if sober, town houses. Highlights of the area include two such patrician mansions, the Museum Van Loon and the Museum Willet-Holthuysen. Medieval

Amsterdam is recalled at the Munttoren, whose base was once part of the Regulierspoort, a gate in the city wall; by contrast, you can see the modern city in full swing in lively Rembrandtplein, formerly a butter market. Opportunities for shopping abound among the antiques of the Spiegelkwartier, at the colourful Bloemenmarkt, and at Albert Cuypmarkt; or catch a movie at Abraham Tuschinski's extraordinary 1921 cinema, now lovingly restored. And you can visit the original Heineken Brewery for a guided tour.

Fish at Albert Cuypmarkt

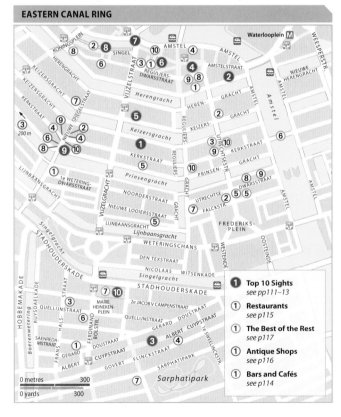

EASTERN CANAL RING

- **1** Top 10 Sights
  see pp111–13
- **1** Restaurants
  see p115
- **1** The Best of the Rest
  see p117
- **1** Antique Shops
  see p116
- **1** Bars and Cafés
  see p114

Interior, Museum Van Loon

1 Museum Van Loon

A chance to see inside a private canal house, whose grand yet welcoming 18th-century interior recreates a bygone age *(see pp36–7)*.

2 Museum Willet-Holthuysen

MAP P6 ▪ Herengracht 605 ▪ 020 523 1870 ▪ Open 10am–5pm Mon–Fri, 11am–5pm Sat, Sun and hols ▪ Closed 1 Jan, 27 Apr, 25 Dec, ▪ Adm ▪ www.willet holthuysen.nl

Though it lacks the lived-in feel of the Museum Van Loon, this 17th-century canal house has its own special atmosphere. An air of stiff formality tinged with melancholy pervades its stately rooms: the Ballroom; the Blue Room, reserved for the men of the house, with painted ceiling by Jacob de Wit; the glittering

Clock, Museum Willet-Holthuysen

Dining Room; and the delicate Garden Room, with views over the formal garden. The collections of its last owners, Louisa Holthuysen and her husband, Abraham Willet, are displayed throughout – paintings, glass, ceramics, silver. The top floor tells the story of the Willets and their art collection. It was the widowed Louisa who left the house and its contents to the city. She died a lonely death in 1885.

3 Albert Cuypmarkt

MAP D6 ▪ Albert Cuypstraat ▪ Open 9am–5pm Mon–Sat ▪ www.albertcuypmarkt.com

Shabby but vibrant, De Pijp is a district where a wide mix of immigrants, artists, students and young couples create a heady atmosphere. Albert Cuypmarkt, which has been trading since 1905, is its bustling hub. The street it occupies, once a canal, was named after Dutch landscape painter Albert Cuyp. With around 260 stalls, backed by all manner of shops and ethnic restaurants, its an unmissable experience. Typically Dutch food stalls – cheese, fish, waffles – jostle merrily with clothes, fabrics, shoes and bags.

4 Rembrandtplein

MAP N6, P6

This former butter market, named after the famous Dutch master painter, has what you might call a split personality. In its centre is a 19th-century statue of Rembrandt set in a tranquil garden, but around its sides are neon-lit, low-brow and, at night, high-octane bars and cafés, packed with Amsterdammers and visitors alike. This is a great place for an early evening drink; try grand cafés NH Schiller *(see p117)* and De Kroon *(see p66)*, as popular at the turn of the 20th century as they are now.

FOAM photography museum

5 FOAM

MAP D5 ■ Keizersgracht 609
■ 020 551 6500 ■ Open 10am–6pm
daily (to 9pm Thu & Fri) ■ Adm
■ www.foam.org

Since it first opened in 2001, FOAM
(short for Fotografiemuseum
Amsterdam) has established an
excellent reputation, displaying the
work of photographers from every
corner of the world, though Dutch
work is often given prominence.
The premises are interesting
too – this was once one of the
city's grandest canal houses.

6 Tuschinski Theater

MAP N6 ■ Reguliersbreestraat
26–34 ■ 0900 1458

Amsterdam's most elaborate cinema
was the extraordinary creation of
Abraham Tuschinski, a self-made
Jewish tailor from Poland. Obsessed
by film and the belief that it could
change lives, he built this cinema in
1921. He later perished in Auschwitz,
but his wonderful creation – termed
Tuschinski Style for its unique mixture

Tuschinski Theater

FLOWER POWER

The Dutch adore flowers, particularly
tulips (**below**). They are everywhere.
You can buy bulbs at the Bloemenmarkt,
visit the vast flower auction at Aalsmeer
and the spring spectacle at Keukenhof,
and cycle through the bulb fields near
Leiden. While you won't find the
mythical black tulip, you can get
something very close to it – a
stunning very dark purple breed
called "Queen of Night".

of architectural influences – lives
on. During an extensive renovation,
hitherto unknown paintings of
Vogue-style ladies were uncovered
and the theatre was returned to its
former glory. Now a Pathé Cinema,
it retains its original charm. Be
sure to buy a ticket for Screen One
to admire the main theatre before
the lights go down.

7 Munttoren

MAP N5

Take a close look at the Mint Tower
(it was briefly used as the city mint
in 1673). Its bottom half is the remnant
of a gate in the medieval city wall.
When the gate burned down in 1618,
Hendrick de Keyser slapped one
of his clock towers on top of the
remains. The carillon of 1699 rings
every 15 minutes. Today, there is a
gift shop on the ground floor.

8 Bloemenmarkt

MAP M5 ■ Singel, between
Koningsplein and Muntplein

Undoubtedly one of Amsterdam's
most picturesque sights, the flower
market is a magnet for tourists.
There are local shoppers too, buying
armfuls for their houses, while

visitors arrange for bulbs to be mailed home. Vendors once sailed up the Amstel from their nurseries to this spot on the Singel, selling their wares directly from their boats. Nowadays, the stalls are still floating, though you wouldn't know it as they feel firmly fixed.

⑨ Spiegelkwartier
MAP D5

In the late 19th century, antique dealers with a sharp eye for an opportunity began to set up shop on Nieuwe Spiegelstraat, leading to the Rijksmuseum. There are more than 80 specialist art and antique dealers in the area now, making it a sparkling, elegant place in which to stroll. Content yourself with looking longingly at the gleaming displays of antique furniture, porcelain and glass, or treat yourself to a faded old Delft tile for just a few euros from Kramer (see p116).

Heineken Experience

⑩ Heineken Experience
MAP D6 ■ Stadhouderskade 78 ■ 020 523 9222 ■ Open Sep–Jun: 10:30am–7:30pm Mon–Thu, 10:30am–9pm Fri–Sun (Jul–Aug: to 9pm daily); last entry at 7pm ■ Adm ■ www. heinekenexperience.com

Heineken's former brewery ceased production here in 1988, but over 18s can still enjoy a free beer at the end of the tour. Learn the story of the famous brewery, walk through the brewhouse with its huge copper stills, and visit the stables. Shire horses still deliver beer (if only for publicity).

EXPLORING THE EASTERN CANAL RING

▶ MORNING

On a fine stretch of the Amstel River, start at dainty **Magere Brug** (see p117). Walking north, follow the river's curve, pausing at **Amstel 104** and its equally crooked neighbours. Reaching **Munttoren**, wander along the **Bloemenmarkt**, then head to Reguliersbreestraat to check out the incredible **Tuschinski Theater**. Its Art Deco interior is worth visiting, even if you don't watch a film here.

Chic Utrechtsestraat, with its appealing selection of restaurants, cafés, delicatessens, boutiques and galleries, is perfect for both shopping and lunch. The best Indonesian *rijsttafel* (see p65) in town is served at **Tujuh Maret** (see p117).

AFTERNOON

From Utrechtsestraat, cross to **Amstelveld**, where the Reguliersgracht intersects picturesquely with Prinsengracht. Make your way along Prinsengracht, cross Vijzelstraat, and dive into Weteringbuurt. On the other side of Prinsengracht, admire elegant **Deutzenhofje** (Nos. 855–899), erected in 1695 for destitute women.

From here, it's only a short walk to the **Museum Van Loon** (see pp36–7), or a little further to **Museum Willet-Holthuysen** (see p111), after which you can wind down with a drink in jolly **Rembrandtplein**.

The Munttoren

See map on p110 ←

Bars and Cafés

1 Het Dwarsliggertje
MAP N6 ▪ Reguliersdwarsstraat 105 ▪ 020 677 8599

The name implies that this understated gay/mixed bar is the street's "sleeper". Indeed, in this street of loud and trendy gay clubs, it has the look and feel of a friendly local.

2 Café van Leeuwen
MAP E5 ▪ Keizersgracht 711 ▪ 020 625 8215 ▪ www.cafevan leeuwen.nl

A beautiful Dutch corner café with a stunning canal view, on the corner of the bustling Utrechtsestraat.

3 De Duivel
MAP N6 ▪ Reguliersdwarsstraat 87

Cypress Hill and The Roots have joined the boisterous baggy brigade at Amsterdam's small but legendary hip hop bar. These days, the hip hop is melted down with anything from funk to disco.

Folk musicians at Mulligans

4 Mulligans
MAP P6 ▪ Amstel 100

If you're tired of the Rembrandtplein, pop round the corner to this Irish bar for some good craic.

5 De Huyschkaemer
MAP E5 ▪ Utrechtsestraat 137 ▪ 020 627 0575

A corner-located, split-level designer bar popular with a young arty crowd. Great atmosphere.

Diners at Kingfisher

6 Kingfisher
MAP D6 ▪ Ferdinand Bolstraat 24 ▪ 020 671 2395 ▪ €

This large and modern bar is one of the best watering-holes in the Pijp. Offers imaginative Dutch and international cuisine.

7 Café Krull
MAP E6 ▪ Sarphatipark 2 ▪ 020 662 0214

Krull is a local favourite, just a few blocks away from the busy Albert Cuyp market. If you feel hungry, there is a good selection of sandwiches on offer.

8 Lellebel
MAP P6 ▪ Utrechtsestraat 4

Amsterdam's infamous – and only – dragshow bar, the complete antithesis of the testosterone-fuelled Rembrandtplein nearby. At first glance it's unremarkable, but when Shirley Bassey is turned up on the soundsystem, the bar staff perform quite some routine.

9 Café Krom
MAP E5 ▪ Utrechtsestraat 76 ▪ 020 624 5343

This 1950s-styled brown café is quickly becoming an Amsterdam tradition. The old jukebox pumps a stream of vinyl nostalgia.

10 Nel
MAP E5 ▪ Amstelveld 12 ▪ 020 626 1199

On a quiet, leafy square, Nel's terrace is the perfect place to relax after a day of wandering the canals.

Restaurants

PRICE CATEGORIES
For a three course meal for one with half a bottle of wine (or equivalent meal), taxes and extra charges.

€ under €30   €€ €30–45   €€€ over €45

1 Warung Spang Makandra
MAP D6 ▪ Gerard Doustraat 39 ▪ 020 670 5081 ▪ €

One of the oldest Surinamese eateries, it serves an array of Indian, Javanese and Surinamese dishes. Try the fried rice with salt cod, or spicy Indian lamb curry with *roti* (flatbread).

2 The Golden Temple
MAP E5 ▪ Utrechtsestraat 126 ▪ 020 626 8560 ▪ €€

Vegetarian restaurant offering a range of Indian, Middle Eastern and Italian food with a home-cooked feel.

3 De Waaghals
MAP D6 ▪ Frans Halsstraat 29 ▪ 020 679 9609 ▪ €€

This restaurant serves organic vegetarian food as well as locally brewed organic wine and beer.

4 Bazar
MAP E6 ▪ Albert Cuypstraat 182 ▪ 020 675 0544 ▪ €€

Cheap and flavourful North African cuisine in the heart of Amsterdam's largest outdoor market, Albert Cuypmarkt *(see p111)*.

5 John Dory
MAP E5 ▪ Prinsengracht 999 ▪ 020 622 9044 ▪ €€€

Set in a 17th-century warehouse, this classic fish restaurant serves creatively prepared fish dishes. The fish served here is caught in the North Sea.

6 Rosa's Cantina
MAP M6 ▪ Reguliersdwarsstraat 38–40 ▪ 020 625 9797 ▪ €€

This Mexican cantina has Tex-Mex down to a tee – the food is varied and delicious – try the excellent *ceviche*, and the margaritas are served in pitchers. Good tequila selection.

7 Bouchon du Centre
MAP E5 ▪ Falckstraat 3 ▪ 020 330 1128 ▪ €€€

Chef Hanneke Schouten cooks fresh produce she's bought from the markets that day, and serves you from her open kitchen. One of the city's best-kept secrets.

8 Utrechtsedwarstafel
MAP E5 ▪ Utrechtsedwarsstraat 107–109 ▪ 020 625 4189 ▪ €€€

Pick a number of courses, choose a range from simple to gastronomic, and leave the rest to the wine connoisseur and cook duo who run this unusual eaterie.

9 Bistrot des Alpes
MAP E5 ▪ Utrechtsedwarsstraat 141 ▪ 020 620 7393 ▪ €€€

Decorated in the style of a French Alpine chalet, this restaurant serves traditional Savoy and other French dishes such as cheese fondue, raclette, and boeuf bourguignon.

10 Zushi
MAP P6 ▪ Amstel 20 ▪ 020 330 6882 ▪ €€

Hyper-modern and hyped-up, this is the place to be if you like your sushi with a zing.

Zushi, a conveyor belt sushi spot

See map on p110

Antique Shops

1 Aalderink Oriental Art
MAP D5 ▪ Spiegelgracht 15

The oldest and most reputable dealer of Asian art and ethnographics in the Netherlands, specializing in fine Japanese *netsuke* (sculptures) and *okimono* (ornaments).

2 Aronson Antiquairs
MAP D5 ▪ Nieuwe Spiegelstraat 45B

David Aronson opened this prestigious gallery around 1900; now it is run by his great-great-grandson. Early Delftware, continental 17th- and 18th-century furniture, plus Chinese *famille verte* and *famille rose* porcelain – much of it rare.

Delftware, Aronson Antiquairs

3 E H Ariëns Kappers / C P J van der Peet BV
MAP D5 ▪ Prinsengracht 677

This shop sells a huge range of mid-16th- to mid-20th-century prints, including remarkable Japanese wood-block prints. By appointment only.

4 Staetshuys Antiquairs
MAP D5 ▪ Nieuwe Spiegelstraat 45A

A curiosity shop selling odd scientific instruments, globes and other unusual objects.

5 Frans Leidelmeijer
MAP D5 ▪ Lijnbaansgracht 369H ▪ 020 625 4627

Frans Leidelmeijer, knighted for his services to the arts, runs this arts and design shop. By appointment only.

6 Bruil & Brandsma
MAP D5 ▪ Nieuwe Spiegelstraat 68

This shop specializes in Dutch folk art and furniture from the past three centuries. The owners are not only interested in the objects, but also in the stories associated with them.

7 Thom & Lenny Nelis
MAP M6 ▪ Keizersgracht 541

A fascinating and unusual collection of medical instruments dating from the early 18th to the early 20th century.

8 Kramer Kunst en Antiek
MAP D5 ▪ Prinsengracht 807

Decorative Dutch tiles, blue Delftware, antique books, prints, pewter, candlesticks and lamps.

9 Gude & Meis Antique Clocks
MAP D5 ▪ Nieuwe Spiegelstraat 60

Stunning rare timepieces – from the earliest bronze to elaborate French ormolu mantel clocks and 17th-century Dutch long-case clocks – can be bought here.

10 Jan Beekhuizen
MAP D5 ▪ Nieuwe Spiegelstraat 49

Deluxe, top-of-the-range antique dealer and valuer with a particularly strong line in furniture and 15th- to 19th-century pewter ware.

Kramer Kunst en Antiek

The Best of the Rest

Magere Brug stretching across the Amstel

1 Tassenmuseum
MAP E4 ▪ Herengracht 573 ▪ 020 524 6452 ▪ www.tassenmuseum.nl
Exhibits in this unique museum of historic bags and purses include a cabinet of rare, brightly coloured 1950s handbags made of "hard plastic", and another of animal handbags in a huge collection, dating as far as the 16th century.

2 Bloemenmarkt
The legendary floating flower market on the Singel *(see pp112–13)*.

3 Concerto
MAP E5 ▪ Utrechtsestraat 52
Simply the best record store in town; new and secondhand.

4 Soup en Zo
MAP D5 ▪ Nieuwe Spiegelstraat 54 ▪ 020 330 7781 ▪ €
This one-stop modern soup kitchen is just a short walk from the Rijksmuseum. Great for takeaways, but some seats are available. Over half the soups are vegetarian.

5 Amstelveld
MAP E5 ▪ Amstelveld
A quiet square tucked away between Utrechtsestraat and Reguliersgracht. There's a wooden church, where concerts are held. Every Monday morning (except in winter), nurseries sell plants, seeds and bulbs.

6 Magere Brug
The city's best-known bridge – worth a wander over the Amstel for perfect photo opportunites, the stunning views, or simply to watch the drawbridge in action *(see p15)*. Romantic at night when it's all lit up.

7 Heineken Experience
If you're here for the beer, this self-guided tour of the original Heineken brewery is a must. Entrance includes three glasses of the famous brew *(see p113)*.

8 The Otherside
MAP M6 ▪ Reguliersdwarsstraat 6 ▪ 020 421 1014
This gay coffeeshop is bright, modern and friendly.

9 NH Schiller
The hotel's brasserie is a gorgeous Art Nouveau escape from touristic Rembrandtplein. Owned for the best part of the last century by painter Frits Schiller, it was a regular meeting place for artists, and still has something of that atmosphere. Schiller's paintings are displayed throughout the premises *(see p146)*.

10 Tujuh Maret
MAP E5 ▪ Utrechtsestraat 73 ▪ €
The city's best Indonesian *rijsttafel*, with vegetarian and meat options.

See map on p110

TOP 10 Museum Quarter

Almond Blossom by Van Gogh

Until the late 19th century, the Museum Quarter lay outside the city limits, a region of small farms and market gardens. Then the city council designated it an area of art and culture, and plans were conceived for the first of Amsterdam's celebrated cultural institutions. With its great museums of art, an internationally renowned concert hall, the city's largest park and a clutch of exclusive shopping streets, the Museum Quarter is today one of Amsterdam's most impressive areas.

MUSEUM QUARTER

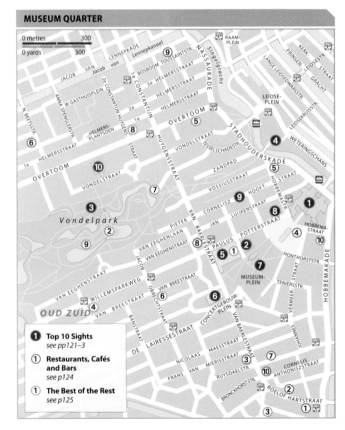

1 Top 10 Sights
  see pp121–3

1 Restaurants, Cafés and Bars
  see p124

1 The Best of the Rest
  see p125

1 Rijksmuseum

Established by King Louis Napoleon in 1808 along the lines of the Paris Louvre, the Rijksmuseum collection has grown in the intervening years to nearly one million works of art. It has moved twice since its beginnings in the Royal Palace on the Dam. Since 1885, it has been housed in P J H Cuypers' ornate Neo-Renaissance building *(see pp16–19)*.

Rijksmuseum

2 Van Gogh Museum

The uncompromisingly modern building by De Stijl architect Gerrit Rietveld was specially designed to display the nation's collection of this disturbed yet brilliant artist's work *(see pp20–23)*.

3 Vondelpark

MAP A6 ▪ Stadhouderskade

Founded in 1864 by a group of philanthropic citizens, this congenial park was later named after the 17th-century poet Joost van den Vondel. Landscaped on informal English lines in 1865 – and enlarged in 1877 – by father and son J D and L P Zocher, with wide green vistas, a profusion of trees and lakes, a rose garden and a bandstand, it became a mecca for hippies in the late 1960s and 1970s. It is still a lively place on summer days, when people flock to hear concerts and plays in the open-air theatre *(see p77)*, glimpse the occasional juggler or fire-eater, jog, rollerblade or play football. There are many different species of plants, trees and wildlife. A distinctive landmark, looking a little like a neat boater turned upside-down, is the round Blauwe Theehuis (Blue Teahouse), built by H A J Baanders in 1936 in the New Functionalist style *(see p125)*.

4 Max Euweplein

MAP C5

Named after the Netherlands' only chess champion, Max Euwe (1901–1981), this square is built on the site of the notorious World War II Huis van Bewaring (House of Detention). It is believed Anne Frank and her family were initially held here after their betrayal. A blue memorial with glass teardrops commemorates this dark passage of history. Nowadays, Max Euweplein has a livelier vibe, with the Hard Rock Café, Comedy Café and Holland Casino all located here. Chess buffs can visit the Max Euwe-Centrum chess museum or partake in a game on the oversized board in the square.

5 Stedelijk Museum

MAP C6 ▪ Museumplein 10 ▪ 020 573 2911 ▪ Open 10am–6pm daily (to 10pm Fri) ▪ www.stedelijk.nl

Devoted to modern art and design from the mid-19th century to the present day, this museum has an impressive collection. The stunning additional wing has increased the exhibition area, as well as creating space for a café and shop *(see p53)*.

Stedelijk Museum

Concertgebouw

6 Concertgebouw

MAP C6 ▪ Concertgebouwplein 10 ▪ 0900 671 8345 ▪ Box office open 1–7pm Mon–Fri, 10am–7pm Sat–Sun ▪ Guided tours 12:30pm Sun, 5pm Mon and Fri ▪ www.concertgebouw.nl

One of the world's great concert halls, the Concertgebouw was built in 1888, designed by A L van Gendt in Neo-Dutch Renaissance style with a colonnaded Neo-Classical façade. In the 1980s, the building was discovered to be in danger of collapse. In time for the centenary of both the concert hall and its world-famous orchestra, new foundations were laid, and the building was restored and enlarged. Amazingly, all this took place without it having to close.

7 Museumplein

MAP C6

The city's largest square was first landscaped in 1872, but it was ruined in 1953 when a hair-raising stretch of road – which locals nicknamed "the shortest motorway in Europe" – was built across it. Completely redesigned between 1990 and 1996, it is now a great swathe of green, still more functional than beautiful, but giving an uninterrupted view from the Rijksmuseum to the Concertgebouw. It has children's play areas and a pond that is frozen over to form an ice-rink in winter. Various events are staged here – from circuses to political demonstrations – and it is the setting for *Hel van Vuur* (Hell of Fire), a monument to all gypsies persecuted by the Nazis, as well as the Ravensbrück Memorial (*see p50*). The district is one of the wealthiest in Amsterdam, with broad streets lined by grand houses.

8 Coster Diamonds

MAP C5 ▪ Paulus Potterstraat 2–8 ▪ 020 305 5555 ▪ Open 9am–5pm daily ▪ www.costerdiamonds.com

Founded in 1840 and now occupying three grand villas, Coster is one of a handful of diamond workshops offering free guided tours. These 30-minute tours give you the opportunity to observe stone graders, cutters and polishers at work. In 1852, the *Koh-i-Noor* (Mountain of Light) diamond was re-polished here for the British Crown Jewels, and a replica of the

DIAMONDS

Amsterdam has been a centre of diamond cutting, polishing and trading since the 16th century (**below**), when Jews, fleeing the Spanish Inquisition, brought the business to the city. The trade flourished in the late 19th century with the influx of Jews from Antwerp, many of them skilled in the industry, and with the import of diamonds from South Africa.

crown that contains it – incorporating a copy of the fabulous blue-white stone – is displayed in the entrance hall. There are diamonds and jewellery for sale here as well as at the Diamond Museum next door.

9 P C Hooftstraat
MAP C5

This elegant shopping street is to Amsterdam what Bond Street is to London. All the names in international fashion are here – Tommy Hilfiger, Hugo Boss, DKNY, Mulberry, Emporio Armani – although well-heeled locals tend to favour friendlier Cornelis Schuytstraat nearby.

De Hollandsche Manege

10 De Hollandsche Manege
MAP B5 ▪ Vondelstraat 140 ▪ 020 618 0942 ▪ Open 10am– 5pm daily (except for three weeks in Aug; check website) ▪ Adm ▪ www. dehollandschemanege.nl

Magnificent and quite unexpected, concealed behind an unexceptional façade, A L van Gendt's Hollandsche Manege is a vast Neo-Classical indoor riding school, built in 1881. (It was commissioned to replace the original Dutch Riding School building, which was situated on Leidsegracht.) Based on the Spanish Riding School in Vienna, it sports elegant plasterwork, sculpted horses' heads, and a stunning open ironwork roof rising high above the sand arena. The school was threatened with demolition in the 1980s but public outcry saved it. If there is a lesson in progress, you can stay and watch. There is also a decent café for high tea.

A DAY IN THE MUSEUM QUARTER

▶ MORNING

Depending on your taste in art, start the day either in the **Rijksmuseum** (see pp16–19) or the **Van Gogh Museum** (see pp20–23). If you choose the former, be selective as the collection is extensive and is spread over four floors of the museum. Whichever museum you visit, you should aim to spend the whole morning there. The Van Gogh Museum has a ground floor café, and you can end your visit with a browse in the museum shop in the entrance hall.

Next, cross **Museumplein** to the **Concertgebouw** and pop in for a look. Make your way to Art Deco **Brasserie van Baerle** (see p124) for lunch. It has a lovely shady garden and is popular, so it's worth booking a table before you set off.

AFTERNOON

Head back to Paulus Potterstraat and **Coster Diamonds**, where you could take one of the half-hour tours. Afterwards, walk along Hobbemastraat until you reach the elegant shops of **P C Hooftstraat**. Turn left and window-shop your way along the boutique-lined street.

If your feet are up to it, spend an hour or so strolling around the **Vondelpark** (see p121), finishing at **Het Blauwe Theehuis** (see p125). Or you could end with a visit to the oldest riding school in the Netherlands, **De Hollandsche Manege**, where young and old can enjoy horse riding. It is open until 5pm everyday.

See map on p120

Restaurants, Cafés and Bars

1 De Bakkerswinkel
MAP C6 ▪ Roelof Hartstraat 68
▪ 020 662 3594 ▪ €

This bakery is an ideal spot for breakfast, lunch or high tea – but beware, it can get crowded.

2 Ferilli's at the College
MAP C6 ▪ Roelof Hartstraat 1
▪ 020 571 1511 ▪ €€€

Brainchild of fashion guru Carlo Ferilli, this classic Italian restaurant is part of the College Hotel, where students master the fine art of hospitality.

3 Brasserie van Baerle
MAP C6 ▪ Van Baerlestraat 158
▪ 020 679 1532 ▪ €€€

This polished contemporary brasserie is popular for its wine list and imaginative French cuisine.

4 Cobra Café
MAP C6 ▪ Hobbemastraat 18
▪ 020 470 0111 ▪ €€

This designer café was created as an ode to the members of the CoBrA art movement. The stylish bar serves delicious cocktails and snacks.

5 Momo
MAP C5 ▪ Hobbemastraat 1
▪ 020 671 7474 ▪ €€€

This Asian-inspired restaurant and lounge is big with the suit-and-tie crowd for its excellent cuisine and sleek interior. An extensive cocktail menu completes the experience.

6 Café de Toog
MAP B5 ▪ Nicolaas Beetsstraat 142 ▪ 020 618 5017 ▪ €€

This congenial café is popular with the locals for its hamburgers, which are made from quality organic beef.

7 Le Garage
MAP C6 ▪ Ruysdaelstraat 54–56 ▪ 020 679 7176 ▪ €€€

The famous and beautiful of Amsterdam fill their tummies and empty their wallets here. The food is a delicate fusion of French with international cuisine.

8 Pompa
MAP C6 ▪ Willemsparkweg 6
▪ 020 662 6206 ▪ €

A warm and friendly eatery offering a three-course menu of Mediterranean fare. Tapas and platters, including the Vegetariano with peppers, tzatziki, hummus and grilled aubergine, are also served.

9 Café Toussaint
MAP J6 ▪ Bosboom Toussaintstraat 26 ▪ 020 685 0737 ▪ €€

This charming, relaxed café-bar has an open kitchen serving delicious lunches and dinners. The romantic terrace is perfect in the summer.

10 Café Wildschut
Roelof Hartplein 1–3
▪ 020 676 8220 ▪ €

Offering an extensive menu, Art Deco interior and a sheltered, south-facing terrace, Café Wildschut has something for everyone.

Barman mixing cocktails at Momo

The Best of the Rest

1 Stedelijk Museum Shop
MAP C6 ▪ Museumplein 10
This treasure trove of a shop is accessible without a ticket to the museum (see p121). It offers an array of books, design items, and gifts for children.

2 Het Blauwe Theehuis
MAP B6 ▪ Vondelpark 5
▪ 020 662 0254
This teahouse in the Vondelpark is one of the city's best-kept secrets, despite its central location (see p66).

3 Harmoniehof
MAP C6
Located near Roelof Hartplein, this tranquil housing estate and garden is a fine example of the Amsterdam School of Architecture.

De Peperwortel

made by littala and Marimekko, as well as, their own brand, &K. They also sell children's toys.

7 Friday Night Skate
MAP C5 ▪ Vondelpark
(Roemer Visscherstraat entrance)
▪ www.fridaynightskate.com
Join this group of skaters for a free, 2-hour, 20-km (12-mile) city tour. Contact them for lessons from 8pm.

8 De Peperwortel
MAP B5 ▪ Overtoom 140
▪ 020 685 1053
This charming *traiteur* is ideally placed for picnicking in the park. Delicious quiches, pasta, salads and soup, with vegetarians well catered for. Plus a choice selection of wine.

Menno Kroon Flower Shop

4 Menno Kroon
MAP B6 ▪ Cornelis Schuytstraat 11 ▪ 020 679 1950
Whether a statuesque bouquet or scented posy, Menno Kroon's floral creations never fail to impress.

5 Marqt
MAP C5 ▪ Overtoom 21
▪ 020 820 8292
Fresh food sourced from local suppliers and independent producers are to be found at this organic store.

6 & Klevering
MAP C6 ▪ Jacob Obrechtstraat 19A ▪ 020 670 3623
Offering an inspiring range of designs, this store sells kitchen and homeware

9 Vondelpark Openluchttheater
MAP B6 ▪ Vondelpark
▪ Jun–Aug: Fri–Sun
Catch a bit of drama, flamenco, pop or puppetry in the Vondelpark's open-air theatre (see p77).

10 Zuiderbad
MAP D6 ▪ Hobbemastraat 26
This restored Art Nouveau swimming pool, dating from 1911, is the city's most stylish place to bathe.

See map on p120

🔟 Plantage

Visitors flock to Amsterdam's excellent zoo, but the rest of this distinguished residential district, with its elegant villas and broad, treelined streets, is often overlooked. Most of the villas appeared in the 19th century, many of them occupied by Jews who had prospered in the diamond industry, and the neighbourhood's strong Jewish tradition is reflected in its numerous memorials. The name "Plantage" means plantation: this was a rural area until the final extension of the Grachtengordel in 1638. Despite its tranquillity, there is no shortage of places to visit and sights to see.

Gilded throne and footstool, Hermitage

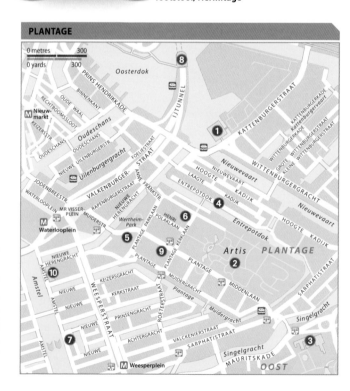

PLANTAGE

1 Het Scheepvaartmuseum

MAP G3 ▪ Kattenburgerplein 1 ▪ 020 523 2222 ▪ Open 9am–5pm daily ▪ Closed 1 Jan, 27 Apr, 25 Dec ▪ Adm ▪ www.hetscheepvaart museum.nl

For anyone who loves ships, the maritime museum is worth a visit. Where sails, ropes and guns were once stored is now an Aladdin's Cave of nautical treasures *(see p53)*. All ages are catered for, with virtual adventures at sea and interactive shows for kids and adults alike. The restaurant and courtyard are open to everyone, not just those visiting the museum.

Het Scheepvaartmuseum

2 Artis Royal Zoo

MAP G4 ▪ Plantage Kerklaan 38–40 ▪ 0900 278 4796 ▪ Open Mar–Oct: 9am–6pm daily (Jun–Aug: to sunset); Nov–Feb: 9am–5pm daily ▪ Guided tours 2pm Sat and Sun ▪ Adm, under 2s free ▪ www.artis.nl

If you want to give human culture a break, this award-winning zoo dates from the 19th century and is the oldest in the Netherlands. About 900 species are kept in reasonably naturalistic surroundings, including an African landscape. Watch the Japanese monkeys grooming one another, the reptiles slithering in their steamy jungle or the only giant anteaters in Holland snuffling for prey. There are plenty of places where you can shelter from the rain, including the Planetarium, Geological and Zoological museums, and the Aquarium, with more than 2,000 fish.

3 Tropenmuseum

MAP G5 ▪ Linnaeusstraat 2 ▪ 088 004 2800 ▪ Open 10am–5pm Tue–Sun ▪ Closed 1 Jan, 27 April, 25 Dec ▪ Adm ▪ www.tropen museum.nl/en

Originally built in 1864 to celebrate Dutch colonialism, Tropenmuseum houses unusual objects from around the world. Set in one of the city's finest historic buildings, the museum mixes ethnography with popular and contemporary art. The separate Tropenmuseum Junior is strictly for 6–13 year olds (no adults unless accompanied by a child).

4 Entrepotdok

MAP G4

The redevelopment of the old VOC warehouses at Entrepotdok has revitalized this dockland area. During the mid-19th century, it was the greatest warehouse area in Europe, being a customs-free zone for goods in transit. The quayside buildings of Entrepotdok are now a lively complex of offices, homes and eateries. Some of the original façades of the warehouses have been preserved, unlike the interiors, which have been opened up to provide an attractive inner courtyard. Outside, brightly coloured houseboats are moored side by side, and herons doze at the water's edge.

Tropenmuseum

Glasshouse, Hortus Botanicus

⑤ Hortus Botanicus
MAP R5 ▪ Plantage Middenlaan 2A ▪ 020 625 9021 ▪ Open 10am–5pm daily ▪ Closed 1 Jan, 25 Dec ▪ Adm ▪ www.dehortus.nl

About 4,000 different species of plants are crammed into this small botanical garden. Many of the exotic plants were collected by the VOC in the 17th and 18th centuries. Highlights are a 300-year old Cycad palm, the three-climates glasshouse and Europe's first coffee plant, smuggled out of Ethiopia in 1706. It also houses a lovely café.

THE DUTCH EAST INDIA COMPANY (VOC)

Amsterdam's wealth in the 17th century was in no small measure due to the success of the VOC (**see its coat of arms below**). Founded in 1602, it had a trading monopoly east of the Cape of Good Hope. Its legendary fleet of "East Indiamen" *(see p61)* carried much of Europe's spice imports until 1791.

⑥ Verzetsmuseum
MAP G4 ▪ Plantage Kerklaan 61A ▪ 020 620 2535 ▪ Open 10am–5pm Tue–Fri, 11am–5pm Sat–Mon, public hols ▪ Closed 27 Apr ▪ Adm ▪ www.verzetsmuseum.org

Following the Dutch Resistance movement from the German invasion in May 1940 to the liberation in May 1945, this interesting exhibition shows how the Dutch people courageously faced the occupation. Its fascinating and evocative displays relate private stories of individual heroism and place them in their historical context. Among the memorabilia are forged identity papers, old photographs and underground newspapers.

Koninklijk Theater Carré

⑦ Koninklijk Theater Carré
MAP F5 ▪ Amstel 115–125 ▪ 0900 252 5255 ▪ Box office open 4–8pm daily ▪ Guided tours 11am Sat ▪ www.carre.nl

This magnificent theatre was built at break-neck speed in 1887 to house Oscar Carré's circus. It has a fine Neo-Renaissance frontage decorated appropriately with the heads of clowns and dancers. Today, it hosts theatre and dance shows, musicals, and even the occasional circus.

⑧ NEMO
MAP F3 ▪ Oosterdok 2 ▪ 020 531 3233 ▪ Open 10am–5:30pm Tue–Sun ▪ Closed Mon except in school hols, 27 Apr, May–Aug ▪ Adm, free for under 3s ▪ www.e-nemo.nl

This popular science and technology centre is the Netherlands' largest.

Green, copper-clad NEMO

It features a range of interactive displays geared towards the entertainment and education of children (see p60). Favourite exhibits include "Soap Bubbles" and "Chain Reaction" on the ground floor, or "Take a journey through the Mind". The 30-m (90-ft), green-copper building, designed by Italian architect Renzo Piano in 1997, resembles the upturned prow of a ship and forms an elevated hood over the road tunnel beneath the River IJ.

⑨ Hollandsche Schouwburg

MAP F4 ■ Plantage Middenlaan 24 ■ 020 531 0310 ■ Open 11am–5pm daily ■ Closed 27 Apr, Yom Kippur, Rosh Hashanah ■ www.jck.nl/en

During the Nazi occupation, this former theatre, now part of the Jewish Historical Quarter, was used as an assembly-point for thousands of Jews. Behind an intact façade, a garden has been created around a basalt monument on the site of the auditorium. Family names of 6,700 Dutch Jews are engraved in a memorial hall to the 104,000 who were exterminated. It is part of the Jewish Historical Quarter.

⑩ Hermitage

MAP Q6 ■ Amstel 51 ■ 020 530 8755 ■ Open 10am–5pm daily ■ Closed 27 Apr, 25 Dec ■ Adm ■ www.hermitage.nl/en

This building, formerly a home for elderly women, now houses a branch of the magnificent State Hermitage Museum in St. Petersburg. Art works from the mother collection are shown at the Amsterdam Hermitage in themed exhibitions.

A DAY IN PLANTAGE

▶ MORNING

Start your day among the cannons, models, figureheads, maps and instruments of the **Het Scheepvaartmuseum** (see p127), then revive yourself at the pleasant ground-floor café. If you secretly hanker after a ship-in-a-bottle, a cutlass paper knife or other objects with a nautical theme, visit the museum shop before you leave. Outside, take a look around the *Amsterdam*, the full-size replica of an 18th-century East Indiaman.

Take a walk down **Nieuwe Herengracht** to the historic **Hortus Botanicus** botanical gardens. Admire the exotic plants in the early 20th-century glass palmhouse and discover some of the rare species collected around the world by the East India Company. Grab lunch at the café.

AFTERNOON

After lunch, you could make your way to Plantage Kerklaan and the **Verzetsmuseum**. A visit here is definitely worthwhile, if harrowing. Afterwards, blow the cobwebs away by spending the rest of the afternoon at **Artis** (see p127). For a few euros, the zoo plan gives you feeding times, as well as pinpointing the two museums and the **Aquarium**. Head back towards the main entrance, where there is a café and a shop selling goods with a wildlife theme. If there is still time left in the day, you could finish your explorations with a quick dash around the solar system at the **Planetarium**.

See map on p126

🔟 Further Afield

Ornamental fountain, Frankendael

Central Amsterdam has more than enough to keep any visitor occupied but, if time permits, the outskirts offer a diverse selection of sights. Football fans will want to make a beeline for the Amsterdam ArenA, home of legendary soccer club Ajax. There are fascinating exhibits on view at the CoBrA Museum, or the EYE Film Institute. If you are interested in architecture, make sure that you visit the Museum Het Schip and the innovative 1920s buildings of De Dageraad housing estate. If it's peace and quiet you want, seek out the small, historic town of Ouderkerk aan de Amstel – older than Amsterdam itself – and the wide open spaces of Het Amsterdamse Bos. The city's excellent transport system makes all these sights easily accessible.

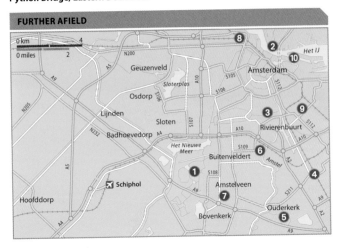

Python Bridge, Eastern Docklands

FURTHER AFIELD

Het Amsterdamse Bos

1 Het Amsterdamse Bos

Bosbaanweg 5 ■ Tram 24; bus 62 ■ 020 545 6100 ■ www.amster damsebos.nl/english

Just a short bus, old-fashioned tram *(see p60)* or bike ride away, this attractive woodland park is a wonderful contrast to the city. Laid out on reclaimed land in the 1930s with the dual purpose of creating jobs for the unemployed and providing more recreation space, the park has woods and meadows, lakes and nature reserves. There is plenty to do: hire bicycles, go boating, eat pancakes, see the bison and the goats and visit the Bos Museum, which describes the park and how it was built.

2 EYE Film Institute

IJpromenade 1 ■ GVB Ferry "Buiksloterweg" (departs from behind Centraal Station) ■ 020 589 1400 ■ Exhibition: open 10am–7pm daily (to 9pm Fri); Box office open 10am–10pm daily (to 11pm Fri–Sat); restaurant/bar: open 10am–1am daily (to 2am Fri–Sat) ■ Adm ■ www.eyefilm.nl/en

The EYE Film Institute Netherlands (previously the Filmmuseum) is located opposite Centraal Station. Designed by Delugan Meissl Associated Architects, this impressive building consolidates a 1,200-sq-m (12,920-sq-ft) exhibition space; four cinemas; an interactive basement showcasing EYE's rich digital collection, with presentations about film history; and installations specifically for children. There's also a well-stocked museum shop.

3 De Dageraad

Burgemeester Tellengenstraat 128 ■ Tram 3, 4 ■ 020 686 8595 ■ Guided tours 11am–5pm Fri–Sun ■ Adm for tours, Visitor's Centre free ■ www.hetschip.nl/en/dageraad

A housing estate seems an unlikely tourist attraction, but the complex built for the De Dageraad (Dawn) housing association from 1918–1923 is well worth a visit – especially for anyone interested in the Amsterdam School of Architecture. Piet Kramer and Michel de Klerk designed sculptural buildings of great originality, with tiled roofs that undulate in waves, and brick walls that billow and curve. The project was part of an initiative to provide better housing for poorer families, in the wake of the revolutionary Housing Act of 1901.

4 Amsterdam ArenA

Arena Boulevard 1 ■ Metro to Strandvliet or Bijlmer Arena; train to Amsterdam Bijlmer Arena ■ 020 311 1333 ■ Tours Jul–Aug: from 10:30am; every 30 minutes (last tour at 4:30pm); Sep–Jun: 10:30am, 11:15am, noon, 12:45pm, 1:30pm, 2:30pm, 3:30pm, 4:30pm daily ■ Adm ■ www.amsterdamarena.nl

Football fans will want to pay their respects to the brilliant Ajax club at their impressive stadium, Amsterdam ArenA. You can take a tour of the state-of-the-art 50,000-seat stadium. There are usually 14 tours a day in summer and 8 in winter, except on event days. The Dutch national team uses the stadium for international practice. Concerts are also held in the ArenA.

Amsterdam ArenA

Ouderkerk aan de Amstel

5 Ouderkerk aan de Amstel

Metro or train to Amsterdam Bijlmer Arena, then bus 300

There was no church in Amsterdam until the 13th century *(see p34)*, so people made the 11-km (7-mile) journey to this riverside village instead to worship at the 11th-century Oude Kerk, which stood here until it was destroyed by a storm in 1674. Convivial waterside cafés and restaurants are the chief lure these days, but you can also walk in the garden of an 18th-century house, Wester Amstel, and visit an unexpected site: the Beth Haim Jewish cemetery. Amsterdam's Jews have been buried here since 1615, when they were forbidden burial in the city.

6 Amstelpark

Europaboulevard ▪ Metro 51 RAI; tram 4; bus 62 ▪ Open dawn–dusk

This welcome green space to the south of the city has a rose garden, a maze and an art gallery, as well as pony rides, farm animals and a miniature steam train for children. At its southern-most tip is the well-preserved De Rieker windmill. Built in 1636, it was a favourite of Rembrandt's, whose statue stands nearby, and is now a private home.

7 CoBrA Museum

Sandbergplein 1–3, Amstelveen ▪ Tram 5 to Binnenhof ▪ 020 547 5050 ▪ Open 11am–5pm Tue–Sun ▪ Closed 1 Jan, 27 Apr, 25 Dec ▪ Adm ▪ www.cobra-museum.nl/en

This museum of modern art in residential Amstelveen is the only museum dedicated to the influential Dutch movement conceived in 1948. Its founders, including Dutchman Karel Appel *(see p49)*, amalgamated the names of their home cities – Copenhagen, Brussels and Amsterdam – to create its name: CoBrA. They wanted to promote art that was spontaneous and inclusive, and were inspired by the work of primitives, children and the men-tally ill. Paintings in the permanent collection are shown in changing thematic displays, augmented by temporary exhibitions. The light, spare building, by Wim Quist, opened in 1995.

8 Museum Het Schip

Spaarndammerplantsoen 140 ▪ Bus 22, 48 ▪ 020 6868 595 ▪ Open 11am–5pm Tue–Sun ▪ Closed 1 Jan, 27 Apr, 25 Dec ▪ Adm ▪ www.het schip.nl

A splendid example of the Expressionist Amsterdam School of Architecture, this municipal housing block takes its name from its ship-like shape. Completed in 1920, it was designed by Michael de Klerk, and is graced by all manner of decorative details – from wavy brick façades to the bulging, cigar-like turret. De Klerk installed a post office in Het Schip and this

CITY OF CYCLISTS

Cycling comes naturally in a country that has more bikes than people. Theft is endemic, so snazzy, expensive models are avoided. Look out for: the huge bike shed at Centraal Station; bikes being dredged up from canals; tourists on yellow bikes; eight-men "conference bikes"; and the heart-shaped "love bike".

now serves as a small museum. Tours take you inside one of the restored residences and up to the turret.

9 Frankendael
Middenweg 72 ▪ Tram 19 ▪ 020 423 3930 ▪ Open noon–5pm Sun; garden open dawn–dusk

South of Plantage Middenlaan, Frankendael Park is Amsterdam's only remaining 17th-century country estate. The elegant Louis XIV-style Frankendael House, ornamental fountain by Ignatius van Logteren, historic formal gardens and coach buildings are all worth seeing. The main building hosts temporary exhibitions and there are two restaurants, the Merkelbach (in the former coach house) and De Kas *(see p65)*. Guided tours of the house take place every Sunday at 2pm.

Eastern Docklands

10 Eastern Docklands
Tram 7, 26; bus 48, 65

A mecca for architecture aficionados, this former docklands area to the east of Centraal Station has been transformed by ambitious urban regeneration plans. Spend a few hours admiring the Python Bridge, inspired by the reptile, or the apartment block that resembles a whale. Also here is a row of houses, each designed by a different architect, and some inspired public art.

A DAY OUT WITH THE KIDS

▶ MORNING

Start by taking tram 7 or 14 to the **Tropenmuseum** *(see p127)*, a fascinating ethnographic museum that explores various non-Western cultures, with an emphasis on former Dutch colonies. Afterwards, enjoy an exotic lunch in the museum's café-restaurant, Ekeko, and don't forget to pop into the gift shop.

AFTERNOON

Outside the Tropenmuseum, pick up tram 7 to the Leidseplein and from there walk through the **Max Euweplein** *(see p121)* – pausing long enough to watch (or play) a giant game of chess – to the **Vondelpark** *(see p121)* where you can take in a music, dance or puppet show at the open-air theatre (in summer). Nearby is the Kinderkookkafé *(Kattenlaantje/Overtoom 325)* where supervised children cook and serve up simple meals.

If park life is a big hit, head to **Het Amsterdamse Bos** *(see p131)*. Be sure to stop at the visitor centre by the main entrance for a map of this sprawling woodland park. Rent bikes or canoes, take a horse-ride or a ride on a historic tram. Don't miss the Fun Forest treetop course, or the working farm where children can pet and feed the animals.

If there is time, take bus 170, 172 or 174 to Amstelveen and end the day with some modern art at the **CoBrA Museum**. Tram 5 or metro 51 will take you back to the city centre.

See map on p130 ←

Streetsmart

Bicycles line a bridge over
a canal in the Jordaan

Getting To and Around Amsterdam

Arriving by Air

Amsterdam Airport Schiphol is efficient, modern and easy to use, with a vast range of facilities from golf to gambling. There is a single – if sprawling – terminal, with one level for arrivals and another level for departures.

The quickest and cheapest method of getting from the airport to the city is by rail. Access to the platforms is by escalator from in front of the train ticket office. Trains run direct to Centraal Station every 4 to 7 minutes from 7am to midnight, then every hour. Journey time is 20 minutes.

Alternatively, the **Connexxion Airport– Hotel Shuttle** bus leaves from outside the airport's main exit. It stops at over 100 hotels, leaving every 30 minutes between 6am and 9pm. You can also take a taxi, but it is hardly worth the expense, considering the ease of public transport.

Arriving by Coach

There are long-distance bus services to Amsterdam from dozens of European cities. Most long-distance buses stop at Duivendrecht Station on the southeast side of the city. From London's Victoria Coach Station, **Eurolines** coaches go to Amsterdam via the Channel Tunnel, taking between 9 and 12 hours in total.

Arriving by Rail

All international and most domestic trains to Amsterdam pull into Centraal Station. The station entrance is on Stationsplein, which is where you will also find Amsterdam tourist information. Trams leave Stationsplein for the rest of the city and regional buses leave from the bus station at the back of Centraal Station beside the River IJ.

Arriving by Road

From the A10 ring road, the S-routes (marked by blue signs) take you to the city centre. Drive on the right. Speed limits are 100 kph (60 mph), 120 kph (75 mph) or 130 kph (80 mph) on motorways, 80 kph (50 mph) outside cities, and 50 kph (30 mph) in built-up areas.

Arriving by Road and Tunnel

To reach Amsterdam by car or motorbike from the UK, you can either take a ferry or use **Eurotunnel**'s shuttle train through the Channel Tunnel from Folkestone to Calais. Advance booking is advised. Amsterdam is roughly 370 km (230 miles) from Calais.

Arriving by Road and Ferry

Three companies operate car ferries from the UK to the Netherlands: **Stena Line** from Harwich to the Hook of Holland (6 hours), 80 km (50 miles) from Amsterdam; **DFDS Seaways** from Newcastle (North Shields) to IJmuiden near Amsterdam (16 hours); and **P&O Ferries** from Hull to Europoort (11 hours), 110 km (70 miles) from Amsterdam.

Arriving by Rail and Ferry

Stena Line, in conjunction with Abellio Greater Anglia trains, operates the Dutchflyer, an inexpensive if somewhat time-consuming rail-and-ferry route from the UK to the Netherlands. Trains depart London's Liverpool Street station bound for Harwich, where they connect with the ferry over to the Hook of Holland (though you can also join the Dutchflyer at stations in between Liverpool Street and Harwich). The whole journey takes between 11 and 12 hours, including the 7-hour ferry crossing. From the Hook, there are frequent trains that journey on to the city of Amsterdam.

Travelling by Tram, Bus, Metro and River Ferry

Operated by **GVB**, Amsterdam's trams and buses cover most of the city – and all the parts you are most likely to visit. Most trams and some city buses start at Centraal Station and they run from

6am (6:30am Sat & Sun) till midnight. A limited night bus service also runs on key routes from midnight to 5:30am.

Amsterdam's metro serves the more outlying parts of the city and has six stations in the centre. Take the Noord/ Zuidlijn (North/South line) from Amsterdam Centraal Station to travel to Rokin, Vijzelgracht and De Pijp. You can also take the Eastern line which stops at Nieuwmarkt, Waterlooplein and Weesperplein.

Behind Centraal Station passenger ferries shuttle across the River IJ; they are all free and there are five routes.

The **OV Chipkaart** (Public Transport Smart-card) is a card that allows you to travel by any means of public transport throughout your stay in the Netherlands. Three cards are available – Personal (reloadable with credit or a season ticket), Anonymous (reloadable with credit only) and Disposable (fixed credit, which includes day passes). When both boarding and alighting, hold the card up to the card reader (either built into the gate or on a free-standing yellow pillar).

By Taxi

Trying to hail a taxi in the street can take a little time – it's often easier to go to one of the city's many taxi ranks. Among others, there are ranks at Centraal Station, Dam Square, Nationale Opera & Ballet, Elandsgracht, Leidseplein, Nieuwmarkt and Rembrandtplein.

By Car

With its complex one-way system, limited parking, canals, trams and cyclists, Amsterdam's centre is not geared up for the motorist. Covered car parks (throughout the city, indicated by a white "P" on a blue background) are the best and cheapest place to leave your car, or make use of the city's Park + Ride network.

On-street parking spaces are hard to find and the city centre is metered every day from 9am until 4am (from noon–4am on Sun). Empty your vehicle of valuables and leave the glove box open after you've parked; foreign-plated cars are often targeted.

By Bicycle

You will never be very far from a bicycle hire shop in this city of cyclists: **Bike City**, **Green Budget Bikes**, and **Macbike** are all conveniently central. Bike theft is rife, so be sure to secure your bike carefully.

By Canal Bike

These two- or four-person pedalos provide a fun way of getting around. There are three central moorings where you can collect or leave the canal bikes all year round.

On Foot

Amsterdam is a great city for walking. The main pedestrian hazards are bicycles, trams, taxis and cobbled streets, so keep clear of cycle lanes, take care crossing tram tracks, and leave heels at home.

DIRECTORY

ARRIVING BY AIR

Schiphol
0900 0141
w schiphol.com

ARRIVING BY COACH

Connexxion
Airport–Hotel Shuttle
w schipholhotelshuttle.nl

Eurolines
w eurolines.co.uk

ARRIVING BY RAIL

Eurostar
w eurostar.com

Eurotunnel
w eurotunnel.com

Nederlandse Spoorwegen (NS)
Dutch national rail
030 751 51 55
w ns.nl

ARRIVING BY ROAD AND FERRY

DFDS Seaways
w dfdsseaways.co.uk

P&O Ferries
w poferries.com

Stena Line
w stenaline.co.uk

TRAMS, BUSES AND METRO

GVB
0900 8011 w en.gvb.nl
w ov-chipkaart.nl

BY TAXI

Taxicentrale
020 777 7777

BY BICYCLE

Bike City
Bloemgracht 68–70
020 626 3721
w bikecity.nl

Green Budget Bikes
Nieuwezijds Voorburgwal 101
020 341 7545
w greenbudgetbikes.nl

Macbike
Stationsplein 5
020 620 0985
w macbike.nl

Practical Information

Passports and Visas

Citizens of the EU/EEA, including the UK and Ireland, plus citizens of Australia, New Zealand, Canada and the USA do not need a visa to enter the Netherlands if staying for 90 days or less, but they do need a current passport.

On the other hand, travellers from many other countries, including South Africa, need a passport and a tourist visa for visits of less than 90 days; visas must be obtained before departure and are available from Dutch embassies.

For stays in the Netherlands of longer than 90 days, EU/EEA residents (with the exception of Bulgarian, Croatian and Romanian nationals) will have few problems, but everyone else needs a mix of visas and permits. Consult your local Dutch embassy before departure.

Customs Regulations and Immigration

Apart from offensive weapons, plants and perishable foods, there are few limits on what EU/EEA nationals can import into the Netherlands for personal use. Non-EU/EEA citizens can buy duty-free goods up to the current limit. Cats and dogs are allowed, provided they have a "Pet Passport", which shows up-to-date inoculations.

Flower bulbs may be exported from the Netherlands; for the USA, a certificate of inspection from the Plant Protection Service is required. Bulbs are best mailed home; the dealer should carry out all the paperwork, but check before you splash out.

Travel Safety Advice

Visitors can get up-to-date travel safety information from the **Foreign and Commonwealth Office** in the UK, the **State Department** in the US and the **Department of Foreign Affairs and Trade** in Australia.

Travel Insurance

It is advisable to take out an insurance policy that covers cancellation or curtailment of your trip and theft or loss of money and baggage. As for medical costs, under reciprocal health arrangements all citizens of the EU/EEA who have a European Health Insurance Card (EHIC) are entitled to discounted medical treatment within the Dutch public health-care system. Non-EU/EEA nationals are not entitled to free or discounted treatment and should take out their own medical insurance – though some countries, for example Australia, do have limited mutual agreements. EU/EEA citizens may also want to consider private health insurance to cover the cost of the discounted treatment as well as items not within the EU/EEA's scheme, such as dental treatment and repatriation on medical grounds. Anyone planning to stay for more than 90 days, even when coming from another EU/EEA member state, is required by Dutch law to take out private heath insurance. When signing up for medical insurance, ascertain whether payment is made prior to, during or after treatment has ended.

Health

Health care in the Netherlands is of an excellent standard and rarely will English speakers encounter language problems – if the doctor or nurse can't speak English themselves there will almost certainly be someone at hand who can. Your local pharmacy, tourist office or hotel should be able to provide the address of an English-speaking doctor or dentist.

If seeking treatment under EU/EEA reciprocal public health agreements, you may be asked to produce documentation to prove you are eligible for EU/EEA health care. Sometimes this is not asked for, but technically at least you should have your passport and your EHIC ready to show.

If you have a travel insurance policy covering medical expenses, you can seek treatment in either the public or private health sectors, the main issue being whether you have to pay the costs upfront and then wait for reimbursement or not. No vaccinations are mandatory for visiting.

Personal Security

Like all major cities, Amsterdam has its share of bag snatchers and pick-pockets, with Centraal Station and the Red Light District being particular hotspots especially late at night. Serious assaults are unusual to rare.

All usual precautions regarding big-city travel apply in Amsterdam: don't flash your wallet, keep an eye on your bag(s), keep valuable items concealed, avoid poorly lit lanes and alleys, and ignore touts offering rooms.

Women travelling alone may well find the Red Light District particularly unpleasant and/or threatening – and whichever sex you are, you can expect grief if you try to photograph the camera-shy prostitutes.

Many tourists buy drugs from on-street dealers, but this is illegal and highly dangerous. In the event that you have anything stolen, obtain a crime report statement or number from the police.

Travellers with Specific Needs

Amsterdam's narrow, cobbled streets, uneven pavements and old buildings with small entrances and steep stairs, make it a difficult city for many disabled people to get around. Similarly, many of the city's hotels are poorly equipped for those with mobility issues, though more modern hotels are often much better. As for public transport, most trams are accessible for wheelchair users, with central doors at pavement level. The metro is wheelchair-friendly, with lifts at every station. For the visually impaired, there is a PA system that announces every stop and the **Dutch Railways (NS)** offers assistance when travelling by train. A folded wheelchair will fit into most taxis, but Amsterdam has a private service, **Boonstra**, specially designed for wheelchair users. It costs the same as a regular cab, but you need to book at least 48 hours in advance.

Most museums have adequate facilities for disabled people, including wide entrances, ramps, lifts and adapted toilets, although canal-house museums like the Van Loon and Willet-Holthuysen have no wheelchair access.

It is possible to get a wheelchair into most ground-floor restaurants, but only a handful have disabled toilet facilities. It is prudent to call ahead to check whether a wheelchair user can be accommodated.

If you need to rent a wheelchair during your stay in Amsterdam, go to the **Accessible Travel Netherlands** website, click on "Assistive Devices" and then "Rent Wheelchair" to make a reservation. If you are planning to use the Dutch rail network and would like assistance on the platform, call the **Bureau Assistentieverlening Gehandicapten** at least 24 hours before your train departs. Dutch Railways publishes information for people with disabilities on their website and in leaflets stocked at all the main train stations.

DIRECTORY

DUTCH EMBASSIES AND CONSULATES

Australia
🌐 netherlands.embassy.gov.au

Canada
🌐 netherlands.gc.ca

Ireland
🌐 embassyofireland.nl

New Zealand
🌐 mfat.govt.nz/netherlands

South Africa
🌐 zuidafrika.nl

UK
🌐 gov.uk/world/netherlands

USA
🌐 usembassy.gov/netherlands

TRAVEL SAFETY ADVICE

Australia (Department of Foreign Affairs & Trade)
🌐 smartraveller.gov.au

UK (Foreign and Commonwealth Office)
🌐 gov.uk/foreign-travel-advice

US (Department of State)
🌐 travel.state.gov

EMERGENCY SERVICES

Police, ambulance and fire
📞 112 or 090 08 844

TRAVELLERS WITH SPECIFIC NEEDS

Accessible Travel Netherlands
🌐 accessibletravelnl.com

Boonstra
Prins Bernhardkade 1, 1165 HL
📞 020 613 4134

Bureau Assistentieverlening Gehandicapten
(Disabled Assistance Office; daily 7am–11pm)
📞 030 235 7822

Dutch Railways (NS)
🌐 ns.nl

Currency and Banking

The currency of the Netherlands is the euro (€), divided into 100 cents. Euro banknotes come in seven denominations: 5, 10, 20, 50, 100, 200 and 500. There are also eight coins: €1 and €2, and 50, 20, 10, 5, 2 and 1 cents. Note that many retailers will not touch the €500 and €200 notes – you have to break them down into smaller denominations at a bank. The prices are rounded off to the nearest 5 cents.

As you might expect, Amsterdam has scores of ATMs and they accept a host of debit cards. Banks often charge a transaction fee for withdrawals. Credit cards can be used at ATMs too, but in this case transactions are treated as loans, with interest accruing daily from the date of withdrawal.

All major debit/credit cards, including American Express, Visa and MasterCard, are accepted in most shops, restaurants and cafés, as well as at ATMs. Typically, Dutch ATMs give instructions in a variety of languages. There are also, Bureaux de Change (Grenswisselkantoor or GWK) at Centraal Station and Schiphol airport, as well as in many of the central squares in town.

Postal Services

Recently privatized (much to the irritation of many Netherlanders), and subsequently rebranded (to even more irritation), the Dutch postal service, **PostNL**, is responsible for the delivery of packages.

PostNL has eschewed traditional post offices and instead their (franchised) services are offered at a large number of newsagents, supermarkets and bookshops – just look out for the orange logo.

Telephone and Internet

The international dialling code for the Netherlands is +31 and the code for Amsterdam is 020, though you drop the first zero of the city code if you are calling from abroad.

Mobile phone (cell phone) coverage in Amsterdam is excellent and it is at GSM900/1800, the band common to the rest of Europe, Australia and New Zealand. Mobile phones bought in North America will need to be able to adjust to this GSM band. Since June 2017, EU nationals travelling within EU are not charged for roaming and pay the same for services as in their home country.

If you are visting from a country outside the EU, and intend to use your phone in the Netherlands, note that call charges can be very high, so check with your supplier before you depart. Text messages, on the other hand, are normally charged at ordinary or at least bearable rates – and with your existing SIM card in place.

You may find it cheaper to buy a Dutch SIM card, though this can get complicated: many providers will not permit you to swap SIM cards (i.e. "unlock" your phone), while others will charge you to do so.

Check with your local service provider before you travel. Furthermore, the connection instructions for the replacement SIM card can be in Dutch only. If you overcome these problems, you can buy SIM cards at high-street phone companies, which offer myriad deals beginning at about €5 per SIM card. If you're unable to unlock your phone, another option is to purchase a pay-as-you-go handset with SIM card after you arrive.

Almost every Amsterdam hotel and hostel as well as most bars, cafés and restaurants offers free internet access. The Dutch phone directory is available (in Dutch) at www.detelefoongids.nl.

TV, Radio and Newspapers

Ask a Dutch child where he or she learned to speak such good, idiomatic English, and the answer is likely to be "from the television". British and American imports on Dutch channels are subtitled rather than dubbed, and cable TV brings around 35 stations from around Europe, plus America's CNN. Most of the city's hotels are equipped with cable TV.

There are several digital radio stations that broadcast various music genres. For classical music, tune in to www.radio4.nl and www.npo3fm.nl for pop music. News is broadcast via www.radio1.nl.

British and American newspapers and magazines are widely available on the day of publication or a day after.

Opening Hours

Normal opening hours for shops and offices are Monday to Friday 8:30am or 9am to 5:30pm or 6pm, and Saturday 8:30am or 9am to 4pm or 5pm, though many larger shops also open late on Thursday or Friday evenings. Sunday opening is becoming increasingly common, with many stores and shops open between noon and 5pm.

Most restaurants open for dinner from about 6pm or 7pm, and though many kitchens close as early as 9:30pm, a few stay open past 11pm and many open for lunch too (from noon to 2pm). Bars, cafés and coffeeshops are either open all day from around 10am or don't open until about 5pm; all close at 1am during the week and 2am at weekends.

Nightclubs generally function from 11pm to 4am during the week, though a few open every night, and some stay open until 5am at the weekend.

Time Difference

The Netherlands is on Central European Time (CET) – one hour ahead of Greenwich Mean Time. Like the rest of the EU and the USA, it observes Daylight Saving Time, so it remains one hour ahead of the UK and six hours ahead of New York throughout the year.

Electrical Appliances

The electricity supply in the Netherlands is 220 volts AC, with standard European-style two-pin plugs. British equipment needs only a plug adaptor; American appliances require a transformer and an adaptor.

Driving

Most foreign driving licences are honoured in the Netherlands, including all EU, US, Canadian, Australian and New Zealand ones. If you are bringing your own car, you must have adequate insurance, preferably including coverage for legal costs, and it's advisable to have an appropriate breakdown policy from your home motoring organization too. To hire a car, you must be 21 or over, with a valid driving licence and a credit card.

Weather

Amsterdam has a temperate climate with moderately cold winters and fairly mild summers. Be prepared for rain at any time of year and don't be surprised if the wind whistles down the canals.

Tourist Information

The **Amsterdam Tourist Information Office** is located opposite Centraal Station on Stationsplein. They provide advice and information on just about everything – including walks, canal tours, sights and exhibitions – and operate an accommodation booking service. Here you can also buy the popular I amsterdam City Card *(see p142)* and the Museumkaart *(see p142)*. Their official website is www.iamsterdam.com, which is a compendious affair with useful, up-to-date information on various accommodations, events, exhibitions, shopping and travel necessary for your stay; you can also book hotel rooms online.

(see p142) ... *(see p142)*

DIRECTORY

POSTAL SERVICES
PostNL
w postnl.post

TELEPHONE AND INTERNET
KPN
w kpn.com

Lebara
w lebara.com

Ortel Mobile
w ortel.nl

T-mobile
w t-mobile.nl

Telephone directory
w detelefoongids.nl

Telfort
w telfort.nl

Vodaphone
w vodaphone.nl

Ziggo
w ziggo.nl

NEWSPAPERS AND MAGAZINES
American Book Center
Spui 12
c 020 625 5537
w abc.nl

Athenaeum Nieuwscentrum
Spui 14–16
c 020 514 1470
w athenaeum.nl

Waterstones
Kalverstraat 152
c 020 638 3821
w waterstones.com/bookshops

TOURIST INFORMATION
Amsterdam Tourist Information Office
Stationsplein
c 020 702 6000
w iamsterdam.com

Shopping

For a medium-sized city, Amsterdam punches well above its weight when it comes to shops and shopping. The main shopping drag is pedestrianized Kalverstraat, which runs south from Dam Square, and this is where you'll find most of the international clothing stores. More distinctive are the cluster of chi chi shops and boutique stores that dot the northern reaches of the Grachtengordel and are collectively known as **De Negen Straatjes** (The Nine Streets).

Also popular, and particularly convenient for the city centre, is the **Magna Plaza** shopping complex, which occupies the old post office just off Dam Square, its several floors crammed with clothing shops.

Amsterdam also clocks up a good range of open-air markets, from the organic food market held on Saturdays on the **Noordermarkt** to the flea market that sprawls over **Waterlooplein** every day except Sunday.

As for specialist shops, the Spiegelkwartier is the heart of the fine art and antiques trade; Gassan is a factory outlet for diamonds; and De Bijenkorf, on Damrak is the city's best department store.

Tax-Free Shopping

Most marked prices include 21 per cent VAT. Global Refund entitles non-EU residents to a percentage back over a minimum figure of €50 (the more you spend, the higher the percentage), bought at one shop on the same day and exported within 90 days. If the shop has "tax-free" status, collect a Global Refund Cheque, have it stamped by Customs on departure, and claim your refund when leaving the EU.

Dining

To cater for its many visitors, Amsterdam heaves with restaurants, everything from cheap and cheerful cafés to the super deluxe. Dutch cuisine is healthy and hearty rather than subtle. Typical street food includes herring in a bread roll with gherkins and (raw) onions in spring and summer and pancakes in autumn and winter.

The city has a plethora of Dutch restaurants, but is more famous for its Indonesian places. Indeed Amsterdam has the finest range of Indonesian restaurants in Europe, reflecting its colonial history as the conqueror of what was long called the East Indies. If you are not familiar with Indonesian food, you may want to start with a *rijsttafel* – a sampler meal consisting of boiled rice and/or noodles served with anything from 10 to 20 small, usually spicy dishes and hot sambal sauce on the side.

Amsterdam is, of course, an international city so there are lots of other cuisines: Italian restaurants are commonplace; Chinese restaurants congregate in Chinatown on the Zeedijk; and Caribbean flavours are available from a number of Surinamese restaurants – Suriname being another former Dutch colony on the South American coast.

Discount Cards

There are a number of cards and passes available to help stretch the holiday budget. The **I amsterdam City Card** represents good value for money, at €57, €67, €77 and €87 for one, two, three or four days respectively. It entitles the holder to free public transport, free admission to many museums, a free canal tour, and discounts at a variety of restaurants and other attractions.

The **Museumkaart** (Museum Card) allows a year's admission to over 400 museums across the Netherlands. On sale at leading Dutch museums, it costs €59.90, or €32.45 for under 18s. Certain museums have no fee for under 18s.

The **Cultureel Jongeren Paspoort (CJP)** gives under 30-year-olds discounted admission to theatres, museums and other attractions. It is available online, and from the offices of the Amsterdam Tourist Board, the AUB Uitburo ticket shop and Stayokay hostels. Prices start at €17.50 for a one-year CJP.

Trips and Tours

The Amsterdam tourist industry makes the most of the city's canals with a veritable armada of glass-topped cruise boats shuttling along the waterways offering everything from quick hour-long excursions to fully fledged longer dinner cruises.

There are several major operators and their jetties are concentrated around Centraal Station, Damrak, and Rokin. Prices for the tours are fairly uniform, with the basic hour-long cruise costing adults €20, children (4–12 years) €10. The big companies also offer more specialized boat trips – literary cruises for example. Note also that the shorter and less expensive cruises are extremely popular and long queues are common.

As an alternative to the standard-issue cruise, several companies offer hop-on, hop-off services from their cruise boats: for example **Lovers'** "Museum Line" hop-on, hop-off boats link most of the city's important museums with a day ticket costing €29.95. There is also a Canal Bus and the Artis Expressboot to the zoo.

There are plenty of tours on dry land too, most temptingly guided cycle rides. A number of companies run guided walks, with guides working for tips only (see p75). **Mee in Mokum** is a well-regarded company whose guided walking tours of the old centre and the Jordaan are provided by long-time Amsterdam residents. Tours run four or five times weekly. Advance reservations required.

For those who prefer pedal power, there is no better city for a cycle tour. With its flat terrain – there's barely any hills to contend with aside from

the arches of canal bridges – and an extensive network of cycle paths and lanes, cycle tours take in all the major sights and allow you to feel a little like a real Amsterdammer. **Yellow Bike** is a long-established company offering guided two- and four-hour bicycle tours for up to 12 people.

Where to Stay

Amsterdam hotels can be pricey, but with so much choice it pays to shop around, especially online. The city has hotels to match every budget from the deluxe to the positively careworn, plus a number of hostels and B&Bs. The choicest area to stay is in the Grachtengordel, the prettiest part of Amsterdam and the area with some of the city's most atmospheric hotels. The worst area is the Red Light District, where the all-pervading seediness is distinctly off-putting. The hotels around Centraal Station and on and near Damrak tend to be functional and relatively inexpensive.

Hotel Rates and Booking

Prices at Amsterdam hotels fluctuate wildly and hit their peak on summer weekends and public holidays, when rooms fill quickly. Most places usually quote room rates rather than prices per person especially as single rooms are increasingly thin on the ground – they are not economic for the hoteliers. Look out for special deals – prices

can be lower if you book a minimum of two nights, for example, especially on weekdays. The best deals are generally available well ahead of time – leave it till the last minute and you can expect to pay through the nose. Websites such as Expedia (www.expedia.com) offer city breaks as well as accomodation.

DIRECTORY

SHOPPING

Magna Plaza
🌐 magnaplaza.nl

De Negen Straatjes
🌐 de9straatjes.nl

Noordermarkt
🌐 noordermarkt-amsterdam.nl

Waterlooplein Flea Market
🌐 waterloopleinmarkt.nl

DISCOUNT CARDS

I amsterdam City Card
🌐 iamsterdam.com

Museumkaart
🌐 museumkaart.nl

Cultureel Jongeren Paspoort (CJP)
🌐 cjp.nl

TOURS

Canal Company
MAP D5
📍 Weteringschans 26
📞 020 217 0500
🌐 canal.nl

Lovers
MAP P1 ■ Prins Hendrikkade 25
📞 020 530 5412
🌐 lovers.nl

Mee in Mokum
📞 020 625 1390
🌐 gildeamsterdam.nl

Yellow Bike
MAP N2 ■ Nieuwezijds Kolk 29
📞 020 620 6940,
🌐 yellowbike.nl

Places to Stay

PRICE CATEGORIES

For a standard, double room per night (with breakfast if included), taxes and extra charges.

€ under €100   €€ €100–200   €€€ over €200

Luxury Hotels

The College Hotel

Roelof Hartstraat 1, 1071 VE ▪ 020 571 1511 ▪ www.thecollegehotel. com ▪ €€

This luxurious "training hotel" for students in the hospitality industry occupies an old school building dating from 1895. The boutique rooms and suites are elegant and include custom-made furniture and Wi-Fi. There is a restaurant, bar and garden for the hotel guests to enjoy.

Hampshire Hotel – Amsterdam American

MAP C5 ▪ Leidsekade 97, 1017 PN ▪ 020 556 3000 ▪ www.hampshirehotel amsterdamamerican.com ▪ €€

This landmark hotel in a splendid 1902 Art Nouveau building with a fountained terrace is for those who want to be close to the action. The glitzy Café Americain is fantastic (see p104).

Amstel InterContinental

MAP F5 ▪ Professor Tulpplein 1, 1018 GX ▪ 020 622 6060 ▪ www. intercontinental.com ▪ €€€

This grand Dutch residence embraces the charm and heritage of the city. Rub shoulders with monarchs and movie stars in Amsterdam's grandest hotel, which oozes opulence, from the spectacular hall to the pampering bedrooms. Enjoy the state-of-the-art gym, and one-Michelin-starred restaurant.

Banks Mansion

MAP N6 ▪ Herengracht 519–525, 1017 BV ▪ 020 420 0055 ▪ www.carlton. nl/banksmansion ▪ €€€

Formerly a bank, this exquisite hotel, successfully fulfills its concept of being a "home from home". Most notably, many of the facilities – internet access, each room's private bar, morning paper and appetisers from the hotel lounge – are all included.

The Dylan

MAP L4 ▪ Keizersgracht 384, 1016 GB ▪ 020 530 2010 ▪ www.dylan amsterdam.com ▪ €€€

Tucked behind the historical façads of Keizersgracht's canal houses, the Dylan Hotel exudes elegance. Contemporary meets classic design, with a manicured courtyard at its heart and a restaurant, Vinkeles, that boasts a Michelin star (see p107).

De l'Europe

MAP N5 ▪ Nieuwe Doelenstraat 2–14, 1012 CP ▪ 020 531 1777 ▪ www.leurope.nl ▪ €€€

Built in 1896, De l'Europe's spacious rooms with empire furnishings are the epitome of plush.

The suites in the Dutch Masters wing are decorated with replicas of masterworks from the Rijksmuseum hand-picked in association with the museum.

Grand Amsterdam (Sofitel Legend)

MAP N4 ▪ Oudezijds Voorburgwal 197, 1012 EX ▪ 020 555 3111 ▪ www.thegrand.nl ▪ €€€

From a 15th-century convent to the Dutch Admiralty headquarters to a former city hall, this hotel boasts a rich history. Offering five-star comfort, it is also home to Michelin star restaurant, Bridges (see p64).

NH Collection Barbizon Palace

MAP P1 ▪ Prins Hendrikkade 59–72, 1012 AD ▪ 020 556 4564 ▪ www.nh-hotels.com ▪ €€€

Behind the façade, a row of 17th-century houses has been knocked together to create this hotel which has a Michelin star restaurant.

NH Grand Hotel Krasnapolsky

MAP N3 ▪ Dam 9, 1012 JS ▪ 020 554 9111 ▪ www.nh-hotels.com ▪ €€€

This monumental hotel, with 469 rooms and 35 apartments, has come a long way from its beginnings as a humble coffeeshop (see p41). The facilities are phenomenal. The original cast-iron and glass Winter Garden breakfast room is nothing short of stunning.

The Toren
MAP L2 ■ Keizersgracht 164, 1015 CZ ■ 020 622 6352 ■ www.thetoren.nl ■ €€€

Graceful but comfortable, this 17th-century canal house has all the modern technology of a luxury hotel. Deluxe rooms have a canal view and a Jacuzzi.

Hotels with Character

Amsterdam Wiechmann
MAP K4 ■ Prinsengracht 328–332, 1016 HX ■ 020 626 3321 ■ www. hotelwiechmann.nl ■ €€

Made from three well-kept canal houses, the Wiechmann has been polishing its welcome for more than 70 years. Wooden floors, beams and panelling set off antique furniture and Oriental rugs throughout the communal areas, and the bedrooms are attractively simple.

Conscious Hotel Vondelpark
MAP A6 ■ Overtoom 519 ■ 020 820 3333 ■ www. conscioushotels.com ■ €€

In a simple modern block a short walk from the Vondelpark, the Conscious Hotel is bright and breezy with large, comfortable and stylishly function rooms. The café, where they serve organic foods, serves breakfast well into the afternoon. There are two Conscious sister hotels nearby.

Hotel Not Hotel
MAP A4 ■ Piri Reisplein 34, 1057 KH ■ 020 820 4538 ■ www.hotelnot hotel.com ■ €€

The quirky rooms in this fun hotel have been imaginatively designed, each with its individual theme. The luxurious bedding and mattresses make up for the smallness of the rooms. Set inside a former market arcade, the communal areas also have character. Kevin Bacon, the hotel bar, is a favourite with locals.

Seven Bridges
MAP E5 ■ Reguliersgracht 31, 1017 LK ■ 020 623 1329 ■ www.seven bridgeshotel.nl ■ €€

A keen bridge-spotter can count seven from this charming hotel. Immaculately decorated, it has wooden floors, Persian carpets and furniture that would grace any auction-house catalogue. There are no public rooms, so you can have breakfast in bed without a twinge of guilt.

Volkshotel Amsterdam Centre
MAP F6 ■ Wibautstraat 150, 1091 GR ■ 020 2612 100 ■ www.volkshotel.nl/ en ■ €€

Located in the former offices of newspaper *De Volkskrant* on the edge of the trendy De Pijp district, the hipster Volkshotel is fun and stylish. The bar on the seventh floor turns into a club in the evening and there is a rooftop mini-spa.

Ambassade
MAP L4 ■ Herengracht 341, 1016 AZ ■ 020 555 0222 ■ www.ambassade-hotel.nl ■ €€€

Truly comfortable and often full, the Ambassade overlooks the mansion-lined Herengracht. Rambling through ten merchant's houses, it blends attractive antiques with modern service. Popular with writers, it has a library with signed copies of their work.

Canal House
MAP L2 ■ Keizersgracht 148, 1015 CX ■ 020 622 5182 ■ www.canalhouse. nl ■ €€€

This hotel brings Dutch art and history into the 21st century. Original timber beams and ornate ceilings sit comfortably in a contemporary setting inspired by the light and dark of traditional Dutch paintings, and rich fabrics of Dutch traders. The restaurant is good value, with excellent food and a garden view.

Hôtel Droog
MAP P5 ■ Staalstraat 7B, 1011 JJ ■ 020 217 0100 ■ www.hoteldroog.com ■ €€€

The eponymous creation of the Dutch design group, this hotel offers spacious rooms on the top floor of their shop and gallery.

Lloyd Hotel
Oostelijke Handelskade 34, 101Q BN ■ 020 561 3607 ■ www.lloydhotel. com ■ €€€

The city's leading design hotel lies in the heart of the gentrified Eastern Docklands. Uniquely, the 117 rooms rank from one-to five-star and have all been individually created by contemporary Dutch designers.

Seven One Seven
MAP E5 ■ Prinsengracht 717, 1017 JW ■ 020 427 0717 ■ www.717hotel.nl ■ €€€

This is a luxuriously laid-back hotel, where beautiful antiques complement the even more beautiful guests. Breakfast, tea and evening drinks are included in the rate.

Family Hotels

Aadam Wihelmina
Koninginneweg 169,
1075 CN ▪ 020 662 5467
▪ www.hotel-aadam-
wilhelmina.nl ▪ €€
This is an excellent two-
star hotel in the Museum
Quarter, with double and
triple rooms. The yellow
breakfast room is particularly jolly. The breakfast
and Wi-Fi are free.

Hotel Arena
MAP G5 ▪ 's Gravesande-
straat 51, 1092 AA ▪ 020
850 2400 ▪ www.
hotelarena.nl ▪ €€
Set in a corner of leafy
Oosterpark, this four-star
hotel is close to the Artis
Royal Zoo (see p127) and
Tropenmuseum. Originally
an orphanage for girls,
the building has been
thoroughly renovated to
offer smartly designed
rooms and suites. While
the rooms facing the park
are especially quiet, the
ones on ground level have
their own little garden.

Max Brown Hotel
Canal Disctrict
MAP M1 ▪ Herengracht
13–19, 1015 BA ▪ 020 522
2345 ▪ www.maxbrown
hotels.com ▪ €€
In a very central location,
this friendly hotel is
housed in three monu-
mental canal houses with
an amazing 300-year-old
façade. The rooms are
decorated with funky
patterns and have all
mod cons.

NH Schiller
MAP N6 ▪ Rembrandtplein
26, 1017 CV ▪ 020 554
0700 ▪ www.nh-hotels.
com ▪ €€
Teenagers might put
up with parents in this

famous Art Deco
hotel overlooking the
Rembrandtplein. There
are plenty of facilities to
keep parents entertained
while the kids explore
the buzzing nightlife.

Owl
MAP C5 ▪ Roemer
Visscherstraat 1, 1054 EV
▪ 020 618 9484 ▪ www.
owl-hotel.nl ▪ €€
Although there are no
particular facilities for
children (beyond triple
rooms, babysitting and
cots for babies), this
family-run hotel in the
Museum Quarter is
noted for its friendliness.
A stuffed owl in an
alcove provides the
name. Rooms are
plain but tastefully
decorated and there
is a pleasant garden.

Rembrandt
MAP F4 ▪ Plantage
Middenlaan 17, 1018 DA
▪ 020 627 2714 ▪ www.
hotelrembrandt.nl ▪ €€
This immaculate,
good-value hotel has
a wonderful antique
breakfast room and
spacious bedrooms
that can sleep up to
six people.

Singel
MAP N1 ▪ Singel 13–17,
1012 VC ▪ 020 626 3108
▪ www.singelhotel.nl
▪ €€
Children who love
animals will enjoy
staying opposite De
Poezenboot (The Cat
Boat; see p14). The
family-run hotel has
an excellent location
on a pretty stretch of
the Singel, and small
but characterful rooms.
Those under the age
of two stay for free.

Albus Hotel
MAP N6 ▪ Vijzelstraat 49,
1017 HE ▪ 020 530 6200
▪ www.albushotel.com
▪ €€€
Parents may prefer
old-world character,
but children usually
like their hotels to
look spanking new,
like this four-star
hotel in the Canal Ring.
Some of the rooms can
accomodate families of
up to four people, and
there is a brasserie for
breakfast and snacks.

Amsterdam House
MAP N5
▪ 's Gravelandseveer 7,
1011 KM ▪ 020 624 6607
▪ www.amsterdamhouse.
com ▪ €€€
Treat the children to
life aboard a houseboat.
Amsterdam House
has eight houseboats
available for short stays
or long-term rental, as
well as apartments and
hotel rooms.

Estheréa
MAP M4 ▪ Singel 303,
1012 WJ ▪ 020 624 5146
▪ www.estherea.nl ▪ €€€
In the same family for
three generations, this
elegant hotel mixes
modern facilities with
traditional surroundings
and a warm atmosphere.
There are family rooms,
some of which overlook
the courtyard, and they
also offer a handy
babysitting service.

Business Hotels

Atlas
MAP C6 ▪ Van
Eeghenstraat 64, 1071 GK
▪ 020 676 6336 ▪ www.
hotelatlas.nl ▪ €€
Friendly and efficient,
though with no particular

business facilities, this Art Nouveau house is near Vondelpark.

Qbic Hotel Amsterdam WTC

WTC, Mathijs Vermeulenpad 1, 1077 XT ▪ 020 238 2195 ▪ www. qbichotels.com ▪ €€
Its location within Amsterdam's World Trade Centre makes this pod hotel ideal for business travellers. Its "cheap chic" concept comes in the form of cube-shaped rooms with mood lighting and a Hästens bed.

Residence Le Coin

MAP N5 ▪ Nieuwe Doelenstraat 5, 1012 CP ▪ 020 524 6800 ▪ www. lecoin.nl ▪ €€
Located in the University District, this smart complex of studios, each with its own kitchenette, is popular with visiting academics.

DoubleTree by Hilton

MAP R2
▪ Oosterdoksstraat 4, 1011 DK ▪ 020 530 0800 ▪ www.doubletree3.hilton. com ▪ €€€
This sleek hotel is the biggest in central Amsterdam. Rooms come equipped with iMac computers and complimentary Wi-Fi. The SkyLounge on the 11th floor offers breath-taking harbour views.

Grand Hotel Amrâth

MAP Q2 ▪ Prins Hendrikkade 108, 1011 AK ▪ 020 552 0000 ▪ www.amrath amsterdam.com ▪ €€€
Merging classic Art Nouveau style with five-star modish comforts, facilities at Grand Hotel Amrâth include board-rooms and banquet halls with AV equipment, and a wellness centre.

Kimpton De Witt Amsterdam

MAP N1 ▪ Nieuwezijds Voorburgwal 5, 1012 RC ▪ 020 620 0500 ▪ www.kimptonde witthotel.com ▪ €€€
This sophisticated, pet-friendly boutique hotel is popular for its excellent facilities for the discerning business traveller. The hotel also hosts social evenings featuring various European wines.

Okura

Ferdinand Bolstraat 333, 1072 LH ▪ 020 678 7111 ▪ www.okura.nl ▪ €€€
Located near the RAI Amsterdam Convention Centre, the Okura offers top-of-the-range luxury and facilities to business travellers. It boasts a minimalist interior integrated with natural wood as well as a brasserie and four restaurants, including the two-Michelin-starred Ciel Bleu on the 23rd floor.

Park Plaza Victoria Amsterdam

MAP P1 ▪ Damrak 1–5, 1012 LG ▪ 020 623 4255 ▪ www.parkplaza.com/ amsterdam ▪ €€€
On the corner of Damrak and opposite Centraal Station, this monumental building has a surprisingly calm and gracious interior. The hotel has a business centre, extensive confer-ence facilities and a health and fitness centre.

Radisson Blu Hotel

MAP N4 ▪ Rusland 17, 1012 CK ▪ 020 623 1231 ▪ www.radissonblu.com/ hotel-amsterdam ▪ €€€
Situated around a dramatic atrium, this well-run hotel comprises several old houses, a paper factory and a 19th-century vicarage, part of which is now a lovely candlelit bar. The health and conference centres are located across the road, connected by a tunnel.

Renaissance Amsterdam

MAP N1 ▪ Kattengat 1, 1012 SZ ▪ 020 621 2223 ▪ www.renaissance amsterdamhotel.com ▪ €€€
A range of facilities at good rates distinguish this central hotel. There are meeting rooms, a business centre and conference centre in a former 17th-century church. The hotel has comfortable rooms, a gym, brown café, boat dock and car park.

Gay-Friendly Hotels

Amistad

MAP L6 ▪ Kerkstraat 42, 1017 GM ▪ 020 624 8074 ▪ www.amistad.nl ▪ €€
Exclusively gay, this old hotel has been vamped up. The rooms are stylish, with red being the predominant colour, and some have shared facilities. Self-catering apartments and pent-houses are also available. Breakfast is served until 1pm, handy if you've been out late the night before at one of the nearby gay clubs and saunas.

For a key to hotel price categories see p144

Amsterdam Hostel Orfeo

MAP D5

■ Leidsekruisstraat 14, 1017 RH ■ 020 623 1347 ■ www.amsterdamhostel orfeo.com ■ €€

While no longer an exclusively gay option, this hostel is in a good location close to Leidseplein and main tourist spots. There is also a fun bar that hosts a great happy hour.

Apartments Unlimited

020 620 1545 ■ www. apartments-unlimited. com/cities/amsterdam ■ €€

Not a hotel but a service offering a variety of accommodation options in central Amsterdam: choose from several studios, apartments, houseboats and an exclusively gay B&B near Amstel River.

Hotel Sander

MAP C6 ■ Jacob Obrechtstraat 69 ■ 020 662 7574 ■ www.hotel-sander.nl ■ €€

A gay-friendly hotel situated behind the Concertgebouw (see p122) in the Museum Quarter. Though plain, most of the 20 rooms are spacious, some with features such as fireplaces and window seats. The breakfast room opens on to a pretty garden.

Mauro Mansion

MAP Q2 ■ Geldersekade 16, 1012 BH ■ 061 297 4594 ■ www.mauro mansion.com ■ €€

Conveniently located near Centraal Station, this lovely boutique hotel welcomes both gay and straight guests. Mauro Mansion's owners, Berry and Marcel, have created a romantic and restful environment. Choose one of the rooms with a canal view.

Quentin

MAP J6 ■ Leidsekade 89, 1017 PN ■ 020 626 2187 ■ www.quentinhotels. com ■ €€

A prime example of an Amsterdam hotel that, although not exclusively gay, extends a warm welcome to its many gay guests. Women in particular make this friendly, well-kept little hotel near Leidseplein their base, as do visiting musicians – popular clubs Paradiso and Melkweg are nearby (see pp70–71).

Quentin England

MAP C5 ■ Roemer Visscherstraat 30, 1054 EZ ■ 020 689 2323 ■ www.quentinengland. com ■ €€

A row of seven unusual houses in this street represents the architec-tural styles of seven different nations. This cosy, gay-friendly establishment occupies two of them; the English cottage and the Netherlands house.

Flower Market Hotel

MAP M5 ■ Singel 458, 1017 AW ■ 065 261 2616 ■ www.flowermarket hotel.com ■ €€€

Bedrooms are a cut above at this smart, gay-friendly hotel within easy reach of the artistic treasures of the Museum Quarter and the historic centre. The distinctive reception room has a black-and-white floor and antique furniture. The famous Bloemenmarkt (see pp112–13) and Leidseplein are both within short walking distance.

Hotel Downtown Amsterdam

MAP L6 ■ Kerkstraat 25, 1017 GA ■ 020 777 6877 ■ www.amsterdam downtownhotel.nl ■ €€€

In the gay enclave of Kerkstraat, this friendly hotel is in a great location. There are 24 bright and clean rooms, and they all come with en-suite facilities.

Quentin Golden Bear

MAP L6 ■ Kerkstraat 37, 1017 GB ■ 020 624 4785 ■ www.quentingolden-bear.com ■ €€€

The Golden Bear welcomes both gay and straight guests. It has been popular since it first opened in 1948. With a pretty façade and 11 clean, neat rooms, some with shared facilities, it's situated in Kerkstraat – a street in the Canal Ring where there are several other gay-friendly venues.

Budget Hotels

Amstel Botel

NDSM Pier 3 (Amsterdam-Noord) ■ 020 626 4247 ■ www. botel.nl ■ €

The idea of staying on a boat in Amsterdam has a certain charm, but the downside of the Amstel Botel is that it isn't moored in central Amsterdam, and the rooms (or cabins if you prefer) on this floating hotel are small. The upside is getting three-star accommodation at a very reasonable price and good views over the harbour. There is also a (free) ferry that will take you to Centraal Station in 10–15 minutes.

Bicycle Hotel Amsterdam
Van Ostadestraat 123, 1072 SV ▪ 020 679 3452 ▪ www.bicyclehotel.com ▪ €€
Clean, cheap, simple rooms away from the tourist traps, with bikes to rent, free maps and advice on routes and sights attract a young clientele. It claims to be 100 per cent climate-friendly, with paper and bottle recycling, and solar panels on the roof. There's also a lounge – of course, what might be a lounge elsewhere is "a chill-out zone" here in De Pijp.

Hegra
MAP L3 ▪ Herengracht 269, 1016 BJ ▪ 020 623 7877 ▪ www.hotelhegra. nl ▪ €€
This 17th-century merchant's house has a prime location on the lovely Herengracht. The Hegra's reasonable prices and the warmth of its welcome make up for the (albeit comfortable) rooms being rather on the small side.

Hermitage Hotel
MAP Q6 ▪ Nieuwe Keizersgracht 16, 1018 DR ▪ 020 623 8259 ▪ www.hotelhermitage amsterdam.com ▪ €€
Situated close to the Amstel, on a peaceful canal, the Hermitage Hotel is clean and well organized. Plump for a room on the top floor, as they have the most

character, but all rooms come with their own shower and toilet.

De Munck
MAP E5 ▪ Achtergracht 3, 1017 WL ▪ 020 623 6283 ▪ www.hoteldemunck. com ▪ €€
Originally built for a ship's captain and within hailing distance of the Amstel, an otherwise traditional interior has been given a dose of 1960s retro. The rooms in the De Munck are airy and clean, and there is also a garden for guest use.

Museumzicht
MAP C5 ▪ Jan Luykenstraat 22, 1071 CN ▪ 020 671 2954 ▪ www.hotelmuseum zicht.nl ▪ €€
You can peer down into the lovely Rijksmuseum garden from the vintage 50s- and 60s-styled rooms at the front of this modest hotel. It occupies the top floors of a Victorian house. The hotel's greatest assets are definitely its splendid location and the great organic breakfasts.

St Christopher's at the Winston
MAP N3 ▪ Warmoesstraat 129, 1012 JA ▪ 020 623 1380 ▪ www.winston.nl ▪ €€
The Winston is located on the doorstep of the Red Light District. This inexpensive art hotel has vibrant rooms, individually designed by local art students. Even the hallways double as exhibition spaces. It attracts a young crowd, in part because of the adjacent club, which

opens from 9pm to 4 or 5am. Breakfast is included.

Travel Hotel Amsterdam
MAP N2 ▪ Beursstraat 23, 1012 JV ▪ 020 626 6532 ▪ www.travelhotel.nl ▪ €€
Though this hotel is very basic, the location of Travel Hotel Amsterdam, in the heart of Oude Zijde and next to the Red Light District, makes up for the lack of facilities. There is also a 24-hour on-site bar to keep hotel guests entertained. A good choice for young night owls on a budget.

Hotel Iron Horse
MAP B5 ▪ Overtoom 33, 1054 HB ▪ 020 262 9220 ▪ www.hotelironhorse. com ▪ €€€
A friendly hotel, housed in a renovated old stable, the Iron Horse is decorated with light colours and features large windows and modern furniture. There are five types of rooms, including: single, double, twin-sharing, triple-sharing, as well as quadruples, with no two rooms the same.

Linden Hotel
MAP C2 ▪ Lindengracht 251, 1015 KH ▪ 020 622 1460 ▪ www.linden hotel.nl ▪ €€€
Occupying a narrow corner among the historical architecture in the Jordaan district, this hotel in a renovated 19th-century building has super-sleek and cleverly designed rooms that come in all shapes and sizes. The Jordaan's plethora of shops and eateries are only a short walk away.

For a key to hotel price categories see p144

Index

Acknowledgments

Main Contributors
Fiona Duncan and Leonie Gass are a British travel-writing team. They are co-authors of three guides in Duncan Peterson's *3-D City Guides* series; *Paris Walks*, in the *On Foot City Guides* series; and several *Charming Small Hotel* guides.

Additional Contributors
Rodney Bolt, Pip Farquharson, Phil Lee

Publishing Director Georgina Dee

Publisher Vivien Antwi

Design Director Phil Ormerod

Editorial Michelle Crane, Rachel Fox, Freddie Marriage, Fíodhna Ní Ghríofa, Scarlett O'Hara, Erin Richards, Sally Schafer

Design Richard Czapnik, Fatima Jamadar, Marisa Renzullo

Commissioned Photography Max Alexander, Clive Streeter, Rough Guides/Natascha Sturny, Rough Guides/Neil Setchfield, Rough Guides/ Roger Norum, Tony Souter

Cartography Mohammad Hassan, Suresh Kumar, Casper Morris

Illustrator chrisorr.com

Picture Research Phoebe Lowndes, Susie Peachey, Ellen Root, Lucy Sienkowska, Oran Tarjan

DTP Jason Little, George Nimmo

Production Stephanie McConnell

Proofreader Leonie Wilding

Indexer Hilary Bird

Revisions Avanika, Rebecca Flynn, Sumita Khatwani, Bhavika Mathur, Alison McGill, Akanksha Siwach, Gerard van Vuuren

Picture Credits
The publisher would like to thank the following for their kind permission to reproduce their photographs:
Key: a-above; b-below/bottom; c-centre; f-far; l-left; r-right; t-top

4Corners: Sandra Raccanello 2tl, 8–9; Maurizio Rellini 3tl, 78–9.

Anne Frank House/AFS: Cris Toala Olivares 11clb, 38cl, 38crb, 38bc, 38–9, 39tl.

akg-images: Herzog Anton Ulrich-Museum / *Dutch Battle Ships* (1683) by Ludolf Backhuysen, Oil on canvas, 76.5 × 8.5cm 33b.

Alamy Images: AA World Travel Library 27bl, 128tl; AGE Fotostock /Alvaro Leiva 87t; Chronicle 44tr; Endless Travel 34bl, 85cla; The Foto Factory 73cl; Hemis /Jean Baptiste 82b, /Ludovic Maisant 65clb; Peter Horree / *Louis Napoleon King of Holland* (1809) by Charles Howard Hodges 44bc; Peter Horree 67tr, 97clb, 106br, 122br, 128cr; imageBROKER / Stephan Gabriel 108t; Eric James 26cla; Kim Kaminski 61tl; Frans Lemmens 36–7, 37br, 105clb, 111tl; LOOK/Ingolf Pompe 64cla; Keese Metselaar 68clb; Daryl Mulvihill 74cr; Alberto Paredes 46br, 124bl; Photempor 100bl; Premium Stock Photography GmbH/Scattolin 103bl; Prisma

Archivo 128bl; Alexei Prokofiev 127br; Jorge Royan 103tr; scenicireland.com/Christopher Hill 76t.

Amsterdam Museum: J. W. Blaeu 11cra; 32t, 33cl, 74tl; René Gerritsen 30cra; Monique Vermeulen 30cl, 30bl, 31cr; Monique Vermeulen AHM 31tr.

Antiekcentrum Amsterdam: 116br.

Aronson Antiquairs: 116ca.

Balthazar's Keuken: 107cra.

Lucas Bols: 69crb.

Café De Jaren: 66tl.

Corbis: 45tr, 87br; Atlantide Phototravel/Massimo Borchi 63b; Van Gogh Museum, Amsterdam/*Portrait of Camille Roulin* (November–December 1888) by Vincent van Gogh 10clb Frans Lemmens 11crb; Jean-Pierre Lescourret 50b, 81cra; Rijksmuseum, Amsterdam/*Marriage Portrait of Isaac Massa and Beatrix van der Laen* (c. 1622) by Frans Hals the Elder 48bl, /*The Merry Family* (1668) by Jan Steen, Oil on canvas. 141 x 110.5 cm (55.5 x 43.5 in). 49cl; Koen Suyk 126cra; The Cover Story/Floris Leeuwenberg 71tr; The Gallery Collection/Museo del Prado, Madrid/*Self-Portrait* (C.1660–1663) by Rembrandt Harmensz. van Rijn 19tl.

De Admiraal: 106cla; **De Hollandsche Manege:** 123cl.; **De Peperwortel:** 125tr.

Dreamstime: Ak4masforest 113clb; Alenmax 57tr; Allard1 131br; Alexis Bélec 1; Vincenzo De Bernardo 75crb; Arthur Bogacki 58t; Artur Bogacki 12br, 13br, 88b, 102tl; Constantinoeite 59tr; David Persson 11br; Matthew Dixon 15crb, 15b; Dutchscenery 4crb, 40b, 81clb; Bernardo Ertl 41cl; Gelyngfjell 80tl; Gpahas 77clb; Hasfanizam 7clb; Instinia Photography 73tr; Isachenka 112cra; Shahid Khan 4clb; Jan Kranendonk 40crb; Veniamin Kraskov 40cla; Ivan Kravtsov 118–19; Giancarlo Liguori 127cl; Tomas Marek 4cra; Miv123 121cla; Msaride 96t; Neirfy 34–5; Olgacov 12cla, 46t, 52bl, 56t, 95tr; *Het Lieverdje* (1959) Carel Kneulman ©DACS (Design And Artists Copyright Society) 2016 89clb; Rognar 54bl; Mario Savoia 130c, 54cl, 55t; Tatuana Sawateeva 54cl; Sborisov 12–13, 54cl, 55t; Sraeva 47tr; Timurk 34cla; Tonyv3112 14t; Anibal Trejo 10cla, 12clb, 28–9; Dennis Van De Water 131tl; VanderWolf Images 129tl; Victormro 11tl; Rudmer Zwerver 6cla.

Eden Amsterdam American Hotel: Peter Baas 104t.

Escape: Klijn Fotografie / Jos Klijn 70t.

Getty Images: AFP/Robin Van Lonkhuijsen 62crb, 77tr; danilovi 3tr, 134–5; De Agostini Picture Library 49tr; DEA /M. Carrieri 48tr, /S. Vannini 95cb; Heritage Images/Van Gogh Museum/ *View of the Prins Hendrikkade and the Kromme Waal in Amsterdam* (1874) by Claude Monet 22tl, /*Saint Geneviève as a Child in Prayer* (1876) by Puvis de Chavannes 22cb; Jasper Juinen 45clb; Christopher Jutting 35crb; Jean-Pierre Lescourret 4bl; Lonely Planet Images 114tr; Stefano Oppo 82cla; Michel Porro 122t; Joe Daniel Price 2tr, 42–3; Josef F. Stuefer 112tl; Mark Venema 62tl.

Greenwoods: 66b.

Het Scheepvaartmuseum: 53crb; Sebastiaan Rozendaal 61b.

Hotel Pulitzer Amsterdam: 109cr.

iStockphoto.com: AleksandarGeorgiev 92–3; dennisvdw 4t; Dutchscenery 4br; Jens Lambert Photography 4cla.

Japanse Winkeltje: 91cla.

Menno Kroon: 125cl.

Museum Van Loon: 36crb, 37tl; Maarten Brinkgreve 36cla; Bert Muller/*Portrait of Willem van Loon in mourning dress* (1636) by Dirck Dircksz. van Santvoort 37c.

Mary Evans Picture Library: Spaarnestad Photo 51tr.

Melkweg: 109bl.

Mulligans: 114clb.

Museum Ons' Lieve Heer op Solder: 88c; Fred Ernst 10br, 24cla, 24clb, 24–5, 25bl.

Olthaar Fotografie: 67cl.

Prik: 68br.

Rijksmuseum: 10cb; *The Milkmaid* (c. 1660) by Johannes Vermeer 16cla; *A Windmill on a Polder Waterway, known as 'In the Month of July'* (c.1889) by Paul Joseph Constantin Gabriël oil on canvas, h 102cm x w 66cm x d 14cm. 16bc; *Isaac and Rebecca, Known as 'The Jewish Bride'* (c. 1665 – c. 1669) by Harmensz. van Rijn Rembrandt 17tr; *Portrait of a Girl Dressed in Blue* (1641) by Johannes Cornelisz Verspronck17cr; *Guanyin, Anonymous*, (1100 – 1200) h 117.0cm × w 111.0cm × d 74.0cm. 18bc; *The Night Watch* (1642) by Rembrandt, oil on canvas, h 379.5 cm × w 453.5 cm 19b; Frans Pegt 16clb.

Robert Harding Picture Library: Amanda Hall 26bc; Kord 59cl; Peter Langer 51cl.

Shop de Ville: 85br.

Spingaren: 99cr.

Stedelijk Museum: John Lewis Marshall 53t, 121br.

TAO group: 70br.

The Movies / FilmHallen: 101t.

Tropenmuseum: 60bc.

Van Gogh Museum, Amsterdam (Vincent van Gogh Foundation): Jan Kees Steenman 7tr; *The Bedroom* (c.1888) by Vincent van Gogh oil on canvas, 72.4 x 91.3cm 20cra; *Wheatfield With Crows* (c.1990) by Vincent van Gogh oil on canvas, 50.5 x 103cm 20clb; *Sunflowers* (c.1888) by Vincent van Gogh, oil on canvs, 92.1 x 73 21tr; *Self Portrait With Grey Felt Hat, Paris*, (September–October 1887) by Vincent van Gogh oil on canvas, 44.5 cm x 37.2 cm, 23tl; *The Yellow House (The Street), Arles* (September 1888) by , Vincent van Gogh, oil on canvas, 72 cm x 91.5 cm 23bl; *Almond Blossom* (1890) by Vincent Van Gogh oil on canvas, 73.3 cm x 92.4 cm120tl.

XtraCold: 69t.

Cover

Front and spine – **AWL Images:** Francesco Iacobelli
Back – **Dreamstime.com:** Olgacov

Pull Out Map Cover
AWL Images: Francesco Iacobelli

All other images © Dorling Kindersley
For further information see: www.dkimages.com

As a guide to abbreviations in visitor information blocks: **Adm** = admission charge; **D** = dinner; **L** = lunch.

Penguin
Random
House

Printed and bound in China

First published in Great Britain in 2003
by Dorling Kindersley Limited
80 Strand, London WC2R 0RL

Copyright 2003, 2018 © Dorling
Kindersley Limited

A Penguin Random House Company

18 19 20 21 10 9 8 7 6 5 4 3 2 1

Reprinted with revisions 2005, 2007, 2009, 2011, 2013, 2015, 2016, 2018

A CIP catalogue record is available from the British Library.

ISBN 978 0 2413 1061 8

MIX
Paper from responsible sources
FSC™ C018179
www.fsc.org

SPECIAL EDITIONS OF DK TRAVEL GUIDES

DK Travel Guides can be purchased in bulk quantities at discounted prices for use in promotions or as premiums. We are also able to offer special editions and personalized jackets, corporate imprints, and excerpts from all of our books, tailored specifically to meet your own needs.

To find out more, please contact:

in the US
specialsales@dk.com

in the UK
travelguides@uk.dk.com

in Canada
specialmarkets@dk.com

in Australia
penguincorporatesales@penguinrandomhouse.com.au

Phrase Book

In an Emergency

Help!	Help!	Help
Stop!	Stop!	Stop
Call a doctor.	Haal een dokter.	Haal uhn dok-tur
Call an ambulance.	Bel een ambulance.	Bell uhn ahm-bew-luhns-uh
Call the police.	Roep de politie.	Roop duh poe-leet-see
Call the fire brigade.	Roep de brandweer.	Roop duh brahnt-vhee

Communication Essentials

Yes	Ja	Yaa
No	Nee	Nay
Please	Alstublieft	Ahls-tew-bleeft
Thank you	Dank u	Dahnk-ew
Excuse me	Pardon	Pahr-don
Hello	Hallo	Hallo
Goodbye	Dag	Dahgh
Good night	Goede nacht	ghoode naht
Morning	Morgen	Mor-ghuh
Afternoon	Middag	Mid-dahgh
Evening	Avond	Ah-vohnd

Useful Phrases

How are you?	Hoe gaat het ermee?	Hoo ghaat het er-may
Very well, thank you.	Heel goed, dank u.	Hayl ghoot, dahnk ew
How do you do?	Hoe maakt u het?	Hoo maakt ew het
That's fine.	Prima.	Pree-mah
Where is/are …?	Waar is/zijn …?	Vhaar iss/zayn
How do I get to …?	Hoe kom ik naar …?	Hoo kom ik naar
Do you speak English?	Spreekt u Engels?	Spraykt ew eng-uhls
I don't understand.	Ik snap het niet.	Ik snahp het neet
I'm sorry.	Sorry.	Sorry

Shopping

How much does this cost?	Hoeveel kost dit?	Hoo-vayl kost dit?
I would like …	Ik wil graag …	Ik vhil ghraakh
Do you have …?	Heeft u …?	Hayft ew
Do you take credit cards?	Neemt u credit cards aan?	Naymt ew credit cards aan
Do you take traveller's cheques?	Neemt u reischeques aan?	Naymt ew raiys-sheks aan
What time do you open/close?	Hoe laat gaat u open/dicht?	Hoo laat ghaat ew opuh/dikht
this one	deze	day-zuh
that one	die	dee
expensive	duur	dewr
cheap	goedkoop	ghoot-koap
size	maat	maat

Types of Shop

antique shop	antiekwinkel	ahn-teek-vhin-kul
bakery	bakker	bah-ker
bank	bank	bahnk
bookshop	boekwinkel	book-vhin-kul
butcher	slager	slaakh-er
cake shop	banketbakkerij	bahnk-et-bahk-er-aiy
cheese shop	kaaswinkel	kaas-vhin-kul
chemist	apotheek	ah-poe-taiyk
delicatessen	delicatessen	daylee-kah-tes-suh
fishmonger	viswinkel	viss-vhin-kul
greengrocer	groenteboer	ghroon-tuh-boor
market	markt	mahrkt
newsagent	krantenwinkel	krahn-tuh-vhin-kul
post office	postkantoor	pohst-kahn-tor
shoe shop	schoenenwinkel	sghoo-nuh-vhin-kul
supermarket	supermarkt	sew-per-mahrkt
tobacconist	sigarenwinkel	see-ghaa-ruh-vhin-kul
travel agent	reisburo	raiys-bew-roa

Sightseeing

art gallery	galerie	ghaller-ee
bus station	busstation	buhs-stah-shown
bus ticket	ov chipkaart	o-vay chip-kaahrt
cathedral	kathedraal	kah-tuh-draal
church	kerk	kehrk
closed on public holidays	op feestdagen gesloten	op fayst-daa-ghuh ghuh-slow-tuh
day return	dagretour	dahgh-ruh-tour
garden	tuin	touwn
library	bibliotheek	bee-bee-yo-tayk
museum	museum	mew-zay-uhm
railway station	station	stah-shown
return ticket	retourtje	ruh-tour-tyuh
single journey	enkeltje	eng-kuhl-tyuh
tourist information	VVV	fay fay fay
town hall	stadhuis	staht-houws
train	trein	traiyn

Staying in a Hotel

Do you have a vacant room?	Zijn er nog kamers vrij?	Zaiyn er nokh kaamers vray
double room	een twee-persoonskamer	uhn tvhay-per-soans-kaa-mer
with double bed	met een twee persoonsbed	met uhn tvhay-per-soans beht
twin room	een kamer met een lits-jumeaux	uhn kaa-mer met uhn lee-zjoo-moh
single room	eenpersoons-kamer	ayn-per-soans-kaa-mer
room with bath shower	kamer met bad douche	kaa-met baht doosh
porter	kruier	krouw-yuh
I have a reservation.	Ik heb gereseveerd.	Ik hehp ghuh-ray-sehr-veert

Eating Out

Have you got a table?	Is er een tafel vrij?	Iss ehr uhn tah-fuhl vraiy
I'd like to reserve a table.	Ik wil een tafel reserveren.	Ik vhil uhn tah-fuhl ray-sehr-veer-uh

breakfast	het ontbijt	het ont-baiyt
lunch	de lunch	duh lernsh
dinner	het diner	het dee-nay
The bill, please.	Mag ik, afrekenen.	Mukh ik ahf-ray-kuh-nuh
waitress	serveerster	sehr-veer-ster
waiter	ober	oh-ber
menu	de kaart	duh kaahrt
starter, first course	het voorgerecht	het vohr-ghuh-rekht
main course	het hoofdgerecht	het hoaft -ghuh-rekht
dessert	het nagerecht	het naa-ghuh-rekht
wine list	de wijnkaart	duh vhaiyn-kaart
glass	het glas	het ghlahss
bottle	de fles	duh fless

Menu Decoder

aardappels	aard-uppuhls	potatoes
azijn	aah-zaiyn	vinegar
biefstuk	beef-stuhk	steak
bier, pils	beer, pilss	beer
boter	boater	butter
brood	broat	bread
cake, taart, gebak	'cake', taahrt, ghuh-bahk	cake, pastry
chocolade	show-coa-laa	chocolate
citroen	see-troon	lemon
cocktail	cocktail	cocktail
droog	droakh	dry
eend	aynt	duck
ei	aiy	egg
garnalen	ghahr-naah-luh	prawns
gebakken	ghuh-bah-ken	fried
gegrild	ghuh-ghrillt	grilled
gekookt	ghuh-koakt	boiled
gepocheerd	ghuh-posh-eert	poached
groenten	ghroon-tuh	vegetables
ham	hahm	ham
haring	haa-ring	herring
hutspot	huht-spot	hot pot
ijs	aiyss	ice, ice cream
jenever	yuh-nay-vhur	gin
kaas	kaas	cheese
kabeljauw	kah-buhl-youw	cod
kip	kip	chicken
koffie	coffee	coffee
kool, rode of witte	coal, roe-duh off vhit-uh	cabbage, red or white
kroket	crow-ket	ragout in breadcrumbs
lamsvlees	lahms-flayss	lamb
mineraalwater	meener-aahl-vhaater	mineral water
mosterd	moss-tehrt	mustard
olie	oh-lee	oil
pannekoek	pah-nuh-kook	pancake
patat frites	pah-taht freet	chips
peper	pay-per	pepper
poffertjes	poffer-tyuhs	tiny buckwheat pancakes
rijst	raiyst	rice
rijsttafel	raiys-tah-ful	Indonesian meal
rode wijn	roe-duh vhaiyn	red wine
rookworst	roak-vhorst	smoked sausage
rundvlees	ruhnt-flayss	beef

schaaldieren	skaahl-deeh-ruh	shellfish
scherp	skehrp	hot (spicy)
schol	sghol	plaice
soep	soup	soup
stamppot	stahm-pot	sausage stew
suiker	souw-ker	sugar
thee	tay	tea
tosti	toss-tee	cheese on toast
uien	ouw-yuh	onions
uitsmijter	ouht-smaiy-ter	fried egg on bread with ham
varkensvlees	vahr-kuhns-flayss	pork
vers fruit	fehrss frouwt	fresh fruit
verse jus	vehr-suh zjhew	fresh orange juice
vis	fiss	fish/seafood
vlees	flayss	meat
water	vhaa-ter	water
witte wijn	vhih-tuh vhaiyn	white wine
worst	vhorst	sausage
zout	zouwt	salt

Numbers

1	een	ayn
2	twee	tvhay
3	drie	dree
4	vier	feer
5	vijf	faiyf
6	zes	zess
7	zeven	zay-vuh
8	acht	ahkht
9	negen	nay-guh
10	tien	teen
11	elf	elf
12	twaalf	tvhaalf
13	dertien	dehr-teen
14	veertien	feer-teen
15	vijftien	faiyf-teen
16	zestien	zess-teen
17	zeventien	zayvuh-teen
18	achttien	ahkh-teen
19	negentien	nay-ghuh-teen
20	twintig	tvhin-tukh
21	eenentwintig	aynuh-tvhin-tukh
30	dertig	dehr-tukh
40	veertig	feer-tukh
50	vijftig	faiyf-tukh
60	zestig	zess-tukh
70	zeventig	zay-vuh-tukh
80	tachtig	tahkh-tukh
90	negentig	nayguh-tukh
100	honderd	hohn-durt
1000	duizend	douw-zuhnt
1,000,000	miljoen	mill-yoon

Time

one minute	een minuut	uhn meen-ewt
one hour	een uur	uhn ewr
a day	een dag	uhn dahgh
Monday	Maandag	maan-dahgh
Tuesday	Dinsdag	dins-dahgh
Wednesday	Woensdag	vhoons-dahgh
Thursday	Donderdag	donder-dahgh
Friday	Vrijdag	vraiy-dahgh
Saturday	Zaterdag	zaater-dahgh
Sunday	Zondag	zon-dahgh

Selected Street Index